DISCARD

Do any of these resonate with you?

- How do I know if my son is ready for kindergarten?
- My daughter struggles to find friends. Should I switch middle schools?
- Homework makes our house a constant battlefield. I'm sick of it.
- My son loves all sports, but his high school doesn't provide many opportunities. Should I consider a different school?
- My child's really shy. Should I homeschool him?
- Ever since another child brought a knife to school, I worry about my child's safety.
- I was a poor student, and my child is heading down the same path. How can I motivate him?
- My friends all have their kids in preschool, and I'm feeling the pressure. But how do I know if it's the right thing for my 3-year-old?
- My son's school friends are really different from the ones he had last year, and his attitude seems to be changing too, for the worse. I'm worried.
- My third grader absolutely hates math. We've tried everything to get him to like it, including a series of tutors. Help!

- I like the idea of specializing my child's education to emphasize areas she's good at, but we can't afford private school. Any ideas?
- I want my child to have the option to get into the best colleges and universities. What educational steps do I need to take along the way to accomplish that?

Education isn't "one size fits all." Nor is it a set menu. I'll show you how to choose schooling options wisely that will provide

- academic excellence
- real-life application
- a perfect match for your child's uniqueness

You *can* have it all.
I guarantee it.

EDUCATION
A LA CARTE

EDUCATION A LA CARTE

CHOOSING
THE BEST SCHOOLING OPTIONS
FOR YOUR CHILD

Dr. Kevin Leman

Revell
a division of Baker Publishing Group
Grand Rapids, Michigan

© 2017 by Dr. Kevin Leman

Published by Revell
a division of Baker Publishing Group
P.O. Box 6287, Grand Rapids, MI 49516-6287
www.revellbooks.com

Printed in the United States of America

Library of Congress Cataloging-in-Publication Data is on file at the Library of Congress, Washington, DC.

ISBN 978-0-8007-2843-4

To protect the privacy of those who have shared their stories with the author, some details and names have been changed.

17 18 19 20 21 22 23   7 6 5 4 3 2 1

To my four grandkids—
Conner, Adeline, Olive, and Ezra.
Don't ever limit yourself—other people
will try to do that for you.
Strive to be your own person.
Tackle obstacles with an attitude of "I can do it."
If you have an opportunity, go after it.
I believe in you. The sky's the limit!
And on top of that,
you're blessed to have great parents.

CONTENTS

9

ACKNOWLEDGMENTS

My grateful thanks to:

- My children in the education field: Holly, Krissy, and son-in-law Dennis.
- The staff of Leman Academy of Excellence.
- My editor and colleague Ramona Cramer Tucker, who shares my passion for excellent education.
- The Revell team.

INTRODUCTION

It's Time to Change the Conversation

Why a quality education is so critical in today's world, and how you can get it.

Every day in America a typical conversation between parent and child plays out something like this:

Parent: "So, what did you learn at school today?"
Child: "Nothin'." (Said with a shrug, turned-away head, or worse, merely a grunt to acknowledge the question was asked.)

What if, instead of that typical exchange, the conversation was a stimulating, lively interaction? One where you as parent wouldn't need to prod for any details? What if, in fact, your child excitedly said, without prompting, "Mom [Dad], guess what I learned at school today!"

Can you imagine such a scene? Well, it *can* happen for you and your child. Not just once but on a continual basis as you find the right schooling match.

Education in general is getting a bad rap these days. Understandably so. According to the National Assessment of Educational Progress, America's high school seniors have shown a decline in math skills in the past three years.[1] ACT scores are also down for 2016. As ACT Chief Executive Officer Marten Roorda says, "When a third of high school graduates are not well prepared in any of the core subject areas, college readiness remains a significant problem that must be addressed."[2] But all the rhetoric about how schools are going down the tubes won't change the course of education unless parents and educators join forces to become a solidified team in shaping quality schooling for today's kids.

It's time we change the conversation about education. School isn't just about cramming information into a child's head, making sure they can recall it so they test well, and getting As that look great on a report card and college transcript. It's about mastering principles that carry into real-life applications. It includes identifying your child's unique skills and interests that encourage her to want to give back to her world.

The quality of education a child receives has everything to do with preparation for life both inside and outside the classroom. As Dr. Bill Bennett, former secretary of education, says, "The essence of education is, in the words of one philosopher, the transmission of civilization—the imparting of ideals as well as knowledge, the cultivation of the ability to distinguish the true and good from their counterfeits, and the wisdom to prefer the former to the latter."[3] However, how much should parents count on teachers and schools to accomplish, and how much should be the role of the parent? And with a growing number of options for schooling, how can parents know what kind of education would be best for their unique child?

Every parent wants their child to be able to compete, and compete well, in a highly dog-eat-dog world that grows more global by the minute. So what does a quality education accomplish?

- It builds a cache of information that, if used with discernment (which is both taught and caught), helps shape thinking that goes on to transform families and culture.
- It prepares today's youth to become healthy, well-balanced individuals in their relationships and all of life.
- It grooms students to become contributing members of society, future leaders, and powerful difference makers in our world.

Why is getting a good education so important? Because schooling isn't just about academic excellence; it's about real-life mastery so your child is groomed for success.

Why am I so passionate about making sure *your* child gets the perfect schooling for her? Because my own educational path was a rock-strewn one. However, my parents—especially my dear, saintly mom (you'll know why I say "saintly" in a minute)—and a teacher who believed in me, as well as finding the right motivation, changed the course of my life.

My Story

I grew up in the Buffalo, New York, area in a very modest home with two working parents whose total income never exceeded $12,000 in any given year. I did poorly in school—so poorly, in fact, that I have a vivid memory of sitting in a first-grade reading group, watching a girl who was eating paste instead of paying attention to her reading. But I also remember thinking, *I know I don't belong in this group. So why am I here?*

Yet I continued to struggle through school, barely eking out any academic existence. It didn't help that I had a straight-A big sister and an older brother who was also a star. I even jokingly referred to him as "God" and got pounded frequently for it by him. So how could I compete? I distinguished myself by getting into trouble in order to be noticed. In fact, I was such a prankster that I drove one of my teachers out of teaching.

It wasn't until April of my senior year in high school that an "older" teacher (she was about 45) pulled me aside and said, "Kevin, have you ever thought of using those skills you have to do something positive in life?"

Skills? I thought, shocked. *I have skills?*

It was the first time I remember a teacher encouraging me by saying I had skills. That moment was eye-opening. Up until then, only two people had truly believed in me—my mother and my father. My mom went out of her way to tell others, "But he's such a good boy," after I'd gotten into trouble once again. Later in life she confessed to me that she used to pray fervently for just one C to appear on my report card as a sign that some potential—*any* potential—was there.

Yet my parents' continued belief in me—who I was and who I would be someday—planted a seed that germinated for years. But it took that teacher, who also tutored me in her home my senior year, to water the seed. I needed both parental involvement and a teacher's highlighting of my skills to make me realize that I did indeed have talents and could go somewhere in life.

But that change didn't happen overnight. I graduated high school fourth from the bottom of my class. My SAT scores were near the 0 percentile. I applied to over 140 colleges and universities, but my high school counselor told me, "Leman, with your grades and record in this school, I couldn't get you admitted to reform school." No school institution wanted me. Even the church denomination I grew up in turned me down for their school.

Finally, nine days before college started, I was admitted on probation to North Park University in Chicago. I managed to eke out a C-minus average my first year. But the prankster in me again kicked in, and the second trimester of my sophomore year, I was thrown out by the dean of students for stealing the "conscience fund." It was really just a college prank gone awry.

Fast-forward 10 years later, though, and I myself was a dean of students at the University of Arizona.

Granted, that's a pretty big leap. "What on earth happened in between?" you ask.

It's simple. I finally found my motivation.

After getting kicked out of North Park University, I moved to Tucson and lived with my parents. I got a job as a janitor in a local hospital.

My life changed one day while I was holding a broom and a five-foot-nine beauty—a nurses' aide—walked by me.

After I found out where she worked in the hospital, I paid the janitor on that unit $5 to introduce me.

That very day I was cleaning the floors in the men's restroom when she walked in to help a little old man go potty. Our eyes met. The first stupid thing I said to my future wife was, "Would you like to go to the World's Fair with me?"

She, being the smarter one of us from the get-go, replied, "I don't know." (The World's Fair was in New York City. We were all the way across the country in Arizona.)

I replied, "How about lunch, then?"

Our first lunch was at McDonald's, where we split a 20-cent cheeseburger and a 10-cent Coke. It was all I could afford.

During that lunch, I fell like a ton of bricks. Through Sande's influence and belief in me combined with my mother's, and a surprising intervention from God Almighty, I gained motivation in my life for the first time. I went back to school, this time at the University of Arizona. Even though I carried a full load of classes and worked part-time, in my very first semester I made the dean's list.

From that point, I never looked back . . . only forward. At last I knew who I was, what I was good at, and how I could use my skills to help families. If my elementary and high school teachers could meet me in person now, I know the vast majority would be shocked that little Kevin Leman amounted to anything. Yet today I have multiple degrees, speak nationally and internationally, and have written over 50 books aimed at helping families thrive.

Because I believe so deeply in the power of education and that every child deserves a quality education uniquely suited to them, I founded Leman Academy of Excellence (www.lemanacademy.com). Based on a classical, rigorous curriculum and my time-tested principles of respect, accountability, and birth order, it's the kind of school that helps students discover their particular niches and prepare for real-life skills, while pursuing excellence as an ultimate long-term goal. By the end of the first grade, our scholars can even diagram a sentence and memorize a poem or narrative that's several paragraphs long and present it in front of the class. And the school upholds the key idea that parental involvement is essential in maximizing the student's educational experience.

Finding the Right Match for Your Child

Back when I grew up, there were no other schooling options for me, other than the school down the block. Clearly the environment and teaching style weren't a match for young Kevin Leman. But that experience developed a deep-seated desire in me as an adult to do everything in my power to ensure that every child is given the opportunity for the right school match. That's what led me to found the swiftly growing Leman Academy and to pen this book.

Parent, one of the most important things you'll ever do is steer your child's education. That's why it's critical you evaluate your child's schooling options carefully.

Today's options on the education menu are many—likely more than you think at this moment. You don't always have to pick just one. You can try a la carte items that are uniquely suited to each individual child as he or she grows.

But where do you start when the options can seem so overwhelming?

You might be thinking about getting your 3-year-old or 4-year-old launched into preschool. You may be wondering if your 5-year-old is ready for kindergarten. Or perhaps you have a fifth grader or middle schooler who is discouraged in her current environment, and you want to try something new. Or maybe you're concerned about your 15-year-old daughter's safety in the school she'd be attending this fall and desire to explore other options.

No matter your situation, *Education a la Carte* will introduce you to a menu of options to consider in your decision. Then you'll want to do further research about the options that look best to you in your specific locale.

You, after all, are your child's most trusted advocate. No one knows your child or her particular bent better. If you choose one direction and realize after a year that it didn't work as well as you'd thought it would, there's nothing wrong with saying, "Let's try something different." Choosing a different direction in education isn't a failure. It's a smart strategy to pursue the best match with your child's present and future in mind.

The type of schooling you pursue for your child is one of the most critical decisions you'll ever make as a parent. That's why you deserve to see and weigh the options for yourself.

In *Education a la Carte*, you'll

- discover what the top concerns of parents are (you're not alone in your fears!)
- learn how to capitalize on your child's strengths, weaknesses, natural talents, and curiosity
- wade through the myriad education options—pros and cons
- understand how your background, expectations, and beliefs influence your definition of success

- find out if your child is ready for preschool or kinder-garten
- gain perspective on grades and homework
- strategize just the right education options for your in-dividual child
- read "What We Did" success stories from parents in the trenches about the schooling options they chose and why

In the "Ask Dr. Leman" section, you'll see the hottest questions parents ask about school-related topics and my time-tested answers. Skim through them as a primer on general issues or read the topics you're currently most concerned about. You can search for other Q&As on my Facebook and podcasts. Having as much information as possible in your hands will help you make a wise decision for each individual child in your family.

If you have a high-flying child, you'll need to become the grounding that child needs as you sort through life's options together.

If you have a child who struggles academically and hates to read, you'll need to become the sleuth who helps figure out how to make education meaningful and targeted.

If you have a child who thinks school is boring, you can work together to figure out how to make it exciting and fun.

If you have a child like me who keeps you guessing with his antics, I know your road seems difficult right now. But I'm living proof of the hope that *anyone* can succeed in life, given the right motivation.

The biggest motivation your child needs is your approval. Knowing you accept him, support him, and believe he is competent to tackle any hurdles he faces in school—yes, even when some evidence seems to point to the contrary—can set his trajectory for the positive in life.

Someday that child will even thank you.

I know that firsthand.

1

The Top Concerns of Parents

What's most important to parents, and how they can best help their child succeed.

I don't have to be in a room long with other parents before they start sharing their concerns with me. Ninety-five percent of the time, those concerns are focused around their children and their long-term welfare. I understand thoroughly, because I'm a parent of five kids who are spaced far enough apart that I was in the active trenches of parenting for a long time. Now I have the joy of being an involved grandparent of four.

Every parent wants the best for their child and will do everything in their utmost power to secure their child's long-term success and happiness. So much of a child's path in life will be determined by the education she receives.

What are your top concerns as a parent? And in an increasingly complicated, fast-paced world, how can you best help your child succeed? Those are million-dollar questions this book will assist you in answering.

Concern #1: Safety at School

These days, parents always list the safety of their children at school as a paramount concern. We live in a violent world, with racial tensions, fear, anger, bullying, and cyberbullying on the rise.

Sadly, shootings in school aren't a new phenomenon, but the scope of the deaths and coverage of them has increased greatly. Why are they so prevalent? A study found that mass killings and school shootings tend to spread "contagiously." In other words, excessive national media coverage of one killing or shooting greatly increases the chance that others—copycats of the crime—will occur within a couple of weeks.[1]

All children crave attention and belonging. Students who haven't had those needs fulfilled in positive ways can easily move toward revenge and begin to identify with the shooters as "celebrities" who have their day in the limelight. The media not only highlights the perpetrator's name, background, and motivation for the crime but also details specifics about weapons used and the number of victims. Effectively, such coverage gives the potential next school shooter a road map for his crime and the hope that he may have his own day in the spotlight.

However, the media coverage of such tragedies also serves to bring the problem to the forefront of our nation's attention.

That allows schools the opportunity to become more prepared for these events. But with the continued occurrence of such tragedies, no school can be completely prepared.

What could possibly make the difference in lessening the number of school shootings? The website Security Today says, "The media needs to eliminate the shooter as the focal point for stories and instead focus on the victims, their families, and highlight what could have been done to prevent this in the first place."[2] In other words, the media should focus not on the shooter—making him into a monster celebrity to be emulated—but on solutions. What can schools do to increase safety and lower the chances of such a shooting happening? What warning signs should students, counselors, and teachers look for? Unfortunately, such coverage isn't likely to happen with the nature of today's media, where the principle of "the more shocking, the more newsworthy the event" reigns.

Many schools have installed extra security precautions—badges for visitors, metal detectors, front security doors, lockdown procedures, regular drills with law enforcement, designated safety areas, and bulletproof classroom doors. They've also trained counselors to spot warning signs and at-risk behavior in students. However, there is no 100 percent guarantee in life, and that includes safety for our children at school. Yes, we can do all in our power to choose the school and its location wisely, but we can't always protect against every aspect of human nature gone awry. Children can be injured or killed while at school, but they also can become victims of drive-by shootings anywhere.

What can be done to limit classroom violence? As Security Today reports, it doesn't matter whether a student is in kindergarten or in college; she will always be at risk because of insufficient security in schools.[3] The best way to limit the risk is to ramp up the resources spent to help troubled students. With bullying so common at school—and cyber-bullying carrying the damage even wider so that the student isn't really safe anywhere, even in his own home where his cell phone accompanies him—school violence and shootings will continue to escalate.

A parent's concerns about the social environment of a school are very valid in terms of safety. Sure, a school may have a strong academic reputation, but what is the atmosphere like? Are the students safe walking the hallways? In the locker rooms? In the restrooms?

When we build Leman Academy of Excellence schools, I make sure every wing has single-unit bathrooms to guarantee privacy. So many problems in school generate from the restrooms. It's a congregating place where not a lot of good happens . . . except for the elimination process. Even if bullying isn't officially allowed, what would the students of the school say confidentially if you asked them? Would they whisper the truth that a certain segment of kids have a "Get out of jail free" card on anything they do, because their parents are heavy hitters with the school administration in some way?

What's the school's internet and social media policy? Is cyberbullying passed over as "just something kids do" and nothing really to be concerned about? Or is it taken seriously and acted upon, involving students, parents, teachers, and administration?

Simply stated, today's school landscape is scary. No school is immune from the fracas, though some schools are more prone to trouble than others. But you as a parent always have a choice of what to do about it.

Concern #2: The Ability to Compete in a Global World

I recently overheard two moms conversing at a doctor's office.

> Mom 1: "I tell him all the time how important school is."
>
> Mom 2 (nodding): "We also stress that she has to get really good grades."
>
> Mom 1: "Agreed. Without them, he won't be able to get into my alma mater. The stipulations for entrance are pretty stiff."
>
> Mom 2: "So what do you think of the Academy on 4th Street, near downtown?"
>
> Mom 1: "I've heard it's an excellent high school. The grads are successful in a lot of different fields. I think Ryan might be good in science."
>
> Mom 2: "Oh? How did you figure that out?"

And the conversation continued.

I couldn't help but shake my head. I looked over at the two little kids sitting on the floor, playing with toys. They weren't even 2 years old yet, and the boy was clearly still in pull-ups.

Yes, we parents need to be proactive. But we also shouldn't go over the top in mapping our child's entire life out when it has barely started.

Let's be honest, shall we? Each one of us wants our child not only to compete but also to be top dog in an increasingly complicated, global world. None of us wants our child on the bottom of the heap if there's anything we can do about it. That means our kids have to be both adequate and skilled in tackling all aspects of technology, which changes at a rapid pace. And they have to do well in subjects we may have done poorly in, such as math and science. Children who aren't, we fear, will be left in everyone else's dust.

> We parents need to be proactive. But we also shouldn't go over the top in mapping our child's entire life out when it has barely started.

That's why we parents, more than at any other time in our history, are pushing our kids. The instant they come into this world, many of us start planning their education and directing their dreams. We talk to them about the importance of school and studying to get good grades before they're even in school or can comprehend what that means.

When friends of ours adopted a baby, they were shocked when other parents told them, "Your baby is already 6 months old and you haven't signed up for kindergarten yet? You're not going to be able to get into one of the best ones. There's a long waiting list."

If you don't have your child in preschool, you've probably faced pressure from other parents who give you "the look." You know, the one that says, "Wow, you really dropped the ball. You're endangering your kid's future."

Why are we so worried that our child becomes a good student? A big motivation is that if they don't get good grades, it means they can't get into a certain college. This pressure transfers to the child psychologically as, "If you don't get into

WHAT WE DID

I have an amazing, delightful daughter, Suzanne. A high-honor student, she has always worked hard on her studies and been self-motivated. Even more important, she willingly gives back to her family and has a compassionate heart toward others. However, when she was a high school senior, she still wasn't certain of her career path. She had interests in engineering, being a pharmacist, or even being an entrepreneur who might start her own company.

After a lot of research together, we decided not to spend the $25,000 per year at the university she'd initially applied to and been accepted at. Instead, Suzanne would take two years of basic classes from the community college nearby. She could save further expenses by living at home for that time. This also would allow her to take a broad variety of classes to fine-tune her direction.

When she was a sophomore, she found her love—genetic engineering. Knowing she could help children who struggled with illnesses completely fit her compassionate heart too. The two years of basic courses from community college transferred directly to the four-year university, so that saved us some more bucks. She's now a senior at the university and loves her internship in genetics. The company, in fact, likes her so much they've offered her a job when she graduates in two months.

Although our plan raised a few eyebrows—including those of my own parents, who couldn't believe we weren't sending our smart daughter straight to university—it was a wise one. It gave Suzanne a running start so she'll be able to exit college with as little debt as possible and with the skills for a solidified career direction that she loves.

that college I want you to get into, then you are a nothing."
But is that the truth?

The reality is that you have to go to some sort of college these days in order to make a decent buck. However, not all students are highly motivated or have the natural skills and intelligence to be accepted by the best colleges in the nation. Pushing them in that direction will only frustrate you and your child. Frankly, most students exit high school with a very fuzzy view of what to do next. If that's the case, then why spend upwards of $100,000 to put your kid through four years of college or a university, earning him a degree he won't know what to do with and doesn't have the passion to really pursue? And incurring debt he or you will be paying off for years to come? The best option might be for him to go to community college for a couple years to get the basic classes covered, and then once he's identified his direction, transfer the credits to a four-year college or university.

Today, college kids have become boomerang kids in huge numbers. When they couldn't find work after graduation, they moved back home. Now they're struggling to find work—any work—that they're passionate about. One 23-year-old I know, Jared, is a sociology major who graduated two years ago from a prestigious four-year university. Problem is, he hasn't been able to identify a single job in the sociology field that sounds interesting to him. He is now majoring in living in his parents' basement and working part-time at a garage to pay the monthly minimum on his college debts. Sadly, this is the same kid who, when he was 16, showed a great deal of interest in auto mechanics. He was always in the garage, tinkering with the clunker car he'd bought for a thousand bucks with money earned from odd jobs. But his parents insisted that he pursue a degree in one of the "helping people" fields—just like his father and grandfather had. Though he often fixed the family car, they didn't see those practical skills as a career direction. Too bad, because auto mechanics seems like a perfect fit for Jared. My guess is that he'll eventually end up in that field, but it'll take him years to pay off his university debts.

Which of you wants to see your child in debt? Or be in debt yourself for years to come? As you think about your child's future college decision, keep your options broad. Is your child more talented with practical skills, such as fixing computers or being a craftsman of some sort? Is she academically focused, someone who would make a good teacher or scientist? In vocational counseling with kids, we always talk about people, data, and things. Does your child show signs that she is specifically interested in one of those three? The answer to those questions—rather than your desire to see your child succeed in a particular way—should become the basis of your brainstorming for your child's future direction. After all, it's not your future. It's hers.

That's why it's important to let your child's natural talents unfold, instead of feeling the push to make her compete in a global world. If your child is in her niche, she will be able to compete. No, she may not be top dog, but that isn't all there is to life.

Parents who fear their kids are going to be left behind are the parents who do their kid's homework and science project. Their reasoning? *He has to have good grades. He has to look good to others or he won't make it in life.*

But think about that for a minute. Do you really have such little confidence that your child can make it on his own? If so, is that because you have little confidence in yourself and you're living with lots of unfulfilled desires? If you as a parent aren't confident, don't expect your child to be. You have to be the one who believes your child can develop what it takes to compete, and compete well, in life and his area of expertise.

Take a look around, parent. Who do you see as successful in life? How did they get there? People who are successful aren't usually those whose path has been snowplowed in life. They're people who have failed, gotten back up, and worked hard toward their dreams because they were internally motivated to make a difference on the planet.

> People who are successful aren't usually those whose path has been snowplowed in life. They're people who have failed, gotten back up, and worked hard toward their dreams because they were internally motivated to make a difference on the planet.

Has your child failed already? What has he learned from you about dusting himself off and getting back up? About working hard? No matter what other teachers your child has, the best teacher of all is you.

Concern #3: The Influence of Peers

Not every child has been raised the way yours has been. Not every child has a parent who cares about her enough to read this book. Parents are wise to consider the influence of peers on their child. As children grow older, peers have a significant impact, especially in the adolescent and teenage years. (If you're in those years, you'll find my books *Planet Middle School* and *Have a New Teenager by Friday* helpful as well.) Those are the years in which your children are figuring out what their parents' values truly are . . . and which of those values they believe themselves. That's why one minute your kids say they love you, and the next they say they hate you. They are simply trying to figure out what is uniquely theirs.

Children who have friends with values similar to their own family's tend to stay with those values in their growing-up years. However, if they never have the opportunity to have their values tested, will they still be able to firmly adhere to them when they are out of your little nest and on their own?

"No way are we sending our child to the regular school in our area," a mom told me recently. "I don't want my daughter around those kinds of people."

Those kinds of people? I thought. *Wow. Nothing like lumping every person in a school in the same category.*

I could relate to her concerns about public schools in general because of all the bad press about them nationally. However, the particular public school she was talking about was a stellar one, with a well-respected administrator who emphasized academic excellence and worked hard to ensure the safest possible environment in his school. She had lumped all public schools and public school kids together.

In the same way, if you're a person of faith, sending your child to a religious school doesn't mean everyone there will share your values. Nor does it mean that you shouldn't be responsible for your own child's religious training at home, where it counts most. Educators are not a replacement for parents.

I understand wanting to protect your kids, but this kind of sad, prejudicial, and short-sighted thinking won't serve your child well. Not sending your child to a certain school so she won't be around certain peers who might make her stray from your values isn't necessarily the answer. Every school has segments of kids who set themselves up to rebel against "the norm." Some rebel quietly; others rebel openly.

There is a gourmet dish called pheasant under glass. In food form, it's a delicious delicacy. But if you try to treat your child like that, you do her a disservice. You might protect her temporarily while she's under the glass. However, as soon as the glass cover is removed, she'll get eaten by the hungry predators that surround her.

Would you intentionally put your child in a dangerous environment? Certainly not. But should you protect her from every idea and worldview that is different from yours? From every bump in the road? Isn't it better that while she still lives at home and you can help her process her choices, she learns to stand strong in whatever environment she is in? That she owns your family's values for herself rather than just accepting them because all of her friends do? That she can navigate the ups and downs of life by herself and gain confidence in doing so? Will you always be there to tell her what she should do and think? To protect her every minute?

All parents have a hidden desire to protect our children as if they're encased in bubble wrap. None of us wants to see our child hurt. But we sometimes take this desire to an extreme.

Jessica's third-grade daughter came home crying because a girl at school told her she was fat. Jessica immediately called the principal and demanded a meeting, then insisted the other girl be expelled. Problem was, Jessica was missing some key details. When the principal informed her that her daughter had called the other girl a bad name first, Jessica was shocked. You see, bullying isn't always one-sided, and children are notorious for leaving out details that might incriminate them.

There is a big difference between bullying and a single negative incident. Kids will always be kids—at times volatile, vindictive, jealous, and even vicious. They'll say and do mean things and won't think of the consequences. But bullying is a repeated pattern of abusive and intimidating behavior that often is based on a clear imbalance of power. In other words, a much larger child is intimidating a much smaller child and taking his lunch money. Or a group of girls is constantly tripping another girl in the hallway by her locker. Onetime negative incidents should be handled by the student participants as much as possible. Yes, an adult should be involved as a backup nearby and within earshot, especially if the incident has involved physical violence, but the resolving of the matter should be between the students, who then have to report the satisfactory resolution to the adult.

In short, peers can have a tremendous influence over your child. As a parent, you should be highly aware of who your child's friends are—and who their parents are. The best way is to naturally involve yourself in your child's world. Volunteer in the classroom or on field trips. Provide snacks for your kids and their friends after school. Nothing draws children into your world better than food. Just hang around within earshot of your kitchen, and you'll learn a lot. Attend concerts and games. Watch who your child interacts with and how she responds.

Especially in the adolescent and teenage years, be aware that your children will experiment with various looks—hairstyles, clothing, makeup, attitudes—on the path to establishing their individuality in the world. That's all very normal. You'll likely go through a lot of those stages with them. As you do, don't major in the minors. Clothing and hairstyles may change from month to month. What matter are your child's heart and attitude. Lauren, one of my daughters, went through a blue-hair phase for a while. But she remained the same kindhearted, others-focused young woman she's always been, so I wasn't worried.

In the tumultuous world of peers—where a BFF one minute can be an enemy the next—what's most important is that your relationship with your child remains constantly loving and supportive. If she can count on you, she won't need to find her identity and belonging among her peers.

Your Home—the Primary School

Throughout your child's life, she will have favorite teachers for various reasons. However, you are the best teacher your child will ever have, and your role is lifelong. What kind of an education is your child getting within your home school, where you are the headmaster? What is your child being taught by watching you? No matter what schooling option you choose, you are your child's primary teacher. Your home is their primary school. Everything and everyone else is secondary.

The type of authority you establish as parent and teacher in your home also sets up the future authority of every teacher your child will have.

Teachers today are bashed physically and F-bombed with regularity in many schools, even by kindergarteners and first graders. Why is that? Because kids haven't been trained by parents to show respect to authority figures. They don't turn in homework because they haven't learned about account-ability and finishing projects they start. They act without consequences because they haven't learned about responsi-bilities and consequences at home.

What values are you teaching at home?

Start with the end in mind.

"Look 10 to 20 years down the road. What do you want your child to be like?" When I ask parents that question, here are some answers that continually pop up:

- To be able to think for herself
- To make good decisions
- To be a person of integrity who does what he says he will
- To be honest and trustworthy
- To care about others
- To work hard and to be able to accomplish her goals
- To not give up, even when times are hard
- To use his skills to better humankind

If that's what you want, then you should "start with the end in mind," as my friend Stephen R. Covey used to say.

Want your child to be able to think for herself and make good decisions? Then allow her to make age-appropriate choices and to experience the consequences—both good and bad—for herself.

Want him to be a person of integrity who is honest and trustworthy? Then if he doesn't get up to make it to school on time, don't rescue him by writing a note that he was at a doctor's appointment. If you want an honest child, then be a role model of honesty in your own life.

Want your child to care about others? Children exit the womb as hedonists, caring only about themselves and their needs. They need to be taught to be considerate of others. Find opportunities where your child can give to others and serve others—whether it's planting flowers in a window box for the elderly woman next door, putting away groceries for her, or helping a younger child who's struggling to learn how to read.

Want your child to work hard and to be able to accomplish her goals, even when the road is hard? Then encourage her to hang in there, even when a task is difficult—such as the geometry she hates. When she's having a difficult time with that clarinet she begged to play, tell her the truth. "It's really hard to learn an instrument, so don't give up. I believe in you. I know you can do it." Don't let her back out of her commitment to band for that year. Many parents have the mentality that their kids should start at the top. But to become truly successful, they need to start at the bottom and work their way up through the challenges.

Want your child to develop skills that can make the planet a better place? Discuss news with her as it occurs. Connect local, national, and international events with her life and increasing skills. For example, "When I volunteered for the class party, I noticed that you were really kind to the new girl in your class. Other kids ignored her, but you included her by asking her to come to your table. Honey, that's wonderful to do, and it made me so happy to see that. If there were more people like you, the news wouldn't be as full of . . ." (and you go on to connect her actions to a recent event). Those types of connections develop global thinking in your child and also prompt her to think, *Hey, all these bad things are happening, but since I'm making a difference in this area right now, maybe I could make an even bigger one when I grow up.* In such a way, you naturally encourage her skills and also grow her heart toward others.

Many parents today tend to overemphasize giftedness. I can't tell you how many times a parent has said to me, "My child is extremely bright and talented."

My usual response? "My condolences."

I say that tongue in cheek, of course. What I mean in all sincerity, though, is that parents shouldn't get caught up in their child's giftedness. Some parents think their kids are exceptional just because they can count from 10 to 1 before kindergarten. Just because your child may be gifted in one area doesn't mean there isn't another child who is more gifted in that area. Allow your child to develop naturally. He will have a lot of years to compete with others in the world. You don't need to jump-start the process.

Throughout your child's education, it's much better that he works at his own pace, doesn't see himself as better than anybody else, and develops positive values that will assist him in becoming the kind of person you want him to be.

Introduce your child to new worlds.

One of the best things you can do is develop a love of reading in your kids. That love starts with you, parent. If your kids are young, make the reading of a bedtime or after-school story part of your routine. Vary the types of books you read. One of your children may love fictional adventures; another may love biographies. You can also share snippets of information or stories you find on the internet.

"I just saw the sweetest story," you tell your second-grade animal-loving daughter, "about baby pandas in China and their caretakers."

She perks up. "Oh yeah? Where?"

You google the site and read the story together. Questions will naturally come up and lead to further research about the animal, the country, and even the living conditions of the average person in China.

Or you say to your sports-loving adolescent, "I wonder what it would be like to win the World Series after 108 years, like the Chicago Cubs did. I don't really understand the rules of baseball. Maybe you can explain it to me sometime." You've given your son the opening to explain to you what he knows. One of the best ways to learn more about something is to teach it to someone else.

> **Learning to read well is as fundamental to being successful in life as learning to dribble a ball is to the game of basketball.**

Learning to read well is as fundamental to being successful in life as learning to dribble a ball is to the game of basketball. As Dr. Bill Bennett says, "The elementary school must assume as its sublime and most solemn responsibility the task of teaching every child in it to read. Any school that does not accomplish this has failed."[4] If you're a good reader, you'll constantly expand your knowledge and assimilate new information. Having a thirst for reading expands your horizons. My grandson, Conner, has read so much about creatures in the ocean and all the planets that

40

he can tell you nearly any detail about them. That love for reading will serve him well in any career he chooses.

Once your child shows interest in specific topics, follow up on those areas. Visit a planetarium or oceanarium, go to the local zoo, attend a free community concert, or go to a local baseball game. Ask friends who have specific jobs—an auto mechanic, a computer programmer, a music teacher, a design consultant, an accountant—to show your child what they actually do. Do the same for your friends' children. You never know what interests you might spark in a young mind.

Make your home the best place to be.

Do you want a child who would rather be with you on a Friday night than with her friends? Who can't wait to return home on her college breaks? Who wants to bring her boyfriend to meet you? Who can't wait for her kids to spend time with their grandparents?

Then start now to make your home the kind of place where all of these elements combine into a one-of-a-kind atmosphere. A place where your child wants to not only show up, but stay and bring her friends to. A place of

- safety and support
- warmth and encouragement
- belonging and acceptance
- growth
- and don't forget the fun!

How can you best help your child succeed in this complicated world? By carefully considering your schooling options in light of your top parental concerns—safety, the ability to compete in a global world, and peer influence. But most of all, by realizing that what happens in the home, with their favorite, lifelong teacher—you—is the most important education they will ever receive.

2

Factoring In Your Child's Uniqueness

Capitalizing on your child's strengths, natural talents, and curiosity.

When I was in eighth grade, I went to see the guidance counselor to get some "guidance" about my future.

"Kevin, what do you want to do when you get older?" he asked.

"I want to be a dentist," I said.

I would have been the worst dentist known to humankind. Why? There's not much perfection in Kevin Leman. *So, I pulled the bicuspid instead of the molar*, I'd think after the fact. *What's the big deal?*

So, you ask, why did I want to be a dentist? Because my orthodontist could talk like Donald Duck, and I thought that was so cool. My interest had nothing to do with my skills or what the job entailed.

Still to this day, I can talk like Donald Duck. In fact, I'm bilingual. I can speak Spanish—*qué pasa*, for "what's up?"—in Donald Duck.

Just because your child says he wants to be a dentist or a fireman or a ballet dancer doesn't mean he truly has a natural bent in that direction. It could be a passing interest due to other factors, like my Donald Duck fetish. Does it mean that you don't investigate those options? Certainly not. It's always good to help your child research his interests. It grows both his knowledge of the larger world and your relationship. Nothing says "I love you" more than choosing to spend time with your child doing what he likes to do. In the midst of the research, whether online or in person, it'll become clear whether that direction is a long-lived one that matches his innate gifts or not.

To get the best education for your child, it's important to know your child's learning style and to discover his unique bent. With that critical information in hand, you can best capitalize on his strengths, natural talents, and curiosity.

Your Child's Learning Styles

There are multiple ways that people learn, and every person tends to use a unique mix of styles. Most traditional classrooms use logical and language-based teaching methods that rely on book-based learning, a lot of repetition, and multiple exams to review, reinforce, and test learning. But there are actually seven different learning styles, and countless combinations of them can occur in any one person.[1]

WHAT WE DID

My daughter, Sydney, has always struggled with memorizing. As soon as she read something and knew she had to memorize it, her brain froze, she said. Then she would cry and ask, "Mom, why am I so dumb? Everybody else can do it, but I can't."

But I knew she wasn't dumb. She just really hated school and felt like a failure. Discovering that there were different learning styles was a big eye-opener for me. I only wish I'd discovered it sooner. The school is really big on memorization and book learning. No wonder Sydney hated it. She's always been musical, ever since she was a toddler. She easily processes anything she hears.

When I identified her learning style as primarily auditory, we put it to the test. We created music for the next poem she had to learn for English class, and she was easily able to memorize it. Seeing her finally smile about anything to do with school made me realize that we needed to make a change. We switched her midyear to a school that was much smaller but catered to children with specific, strong learning styles.

That was two years ago. Not only is Sydney thriving in her current school and her relationships there, but she's learned two additional musical instruments and is interested in pursuing a career as a music teacher. The switch has been a win-win for all!

- Visual/spatial: Your child learns through what he sees, such as images and pictures.
- Auditory/musical: Your child learns through sound, such as music and hearing a concept explained.

- Verbal/linguistic: Your child learns through words, both in writing and in speech.
- Kinesthetic/physical: Your child learns through physical motion and the sense of touch.
- Logical/mathematical: Your child learns through logic and reasoning.
- Social/interpersonal: Your child learns by working in groups and with other people.
- Solitary/intrapersonal: Your child learns by working alone.

Think through each of these learning styles. Can you identify which ones best suit your child? Does she need images? Music? Words? Physical movement? Logic? Does he work best by himself or in groups?

If your child was going to learn something new, how would he learn best? If you don't know, try out a few options for fun. Show pictures, play some music, and have him sit solo or in a group, and you'll get a basic idea of his learning styles.

Recognizing the ways your child learns will greatly help you in identifying the best learning environment for his particular needs. If he learns primarily through physical motion, he won't do well in a traditional classroom where he'll have to sit for hours. If he can't study by himself, he won't do well in an online or virtual classroom. If he needs to work in groups and you're homeschooling him by himself, you'd be wise to broaden his education to include group work on specific subjects or some larger classroom experience. See how this wonderful knowledge of learning styles can work to your advantage and your child's?

Your Child's Natural Bent

I spoke earlier of my bilingual gifts—Donald Duck and a smattering of Spanish—mainly from living in Tucson, Arizona, where some of the street names are a mouthful. When I was in eighth grade, I brought home a future schedule of classes to take as a freshman in high school. My dad saw Latin 1 listed on it. His only knowledge of Latin came from the Catholic Church, where most of the Mass was spoken in that language. A blue-collar worker who had only graduated from the eighth grade himself, Dad didn't have the wherewithal to say, "What on earth are you taking that for? Especially with your barely passing grades in school?" As far as he was concerned, "Latin 1" might as well have said "Swahili 1." He just gave it a passing glance.

By the way, I did take Latin 1. I only passed the class because a fellow student was kind enough to lower his left shoulder during our final exam. Otherwise, I'd still be in Latin 1. I took Latin 2 three times, flunking it twice.

Just because I filled in the blank with a class that looked interesting didn't mean I thought I might be good at it. Clearly I wasn't naturally gifted in languages, but I didn't really have anyone to help me sort through the options.

How do you identify the areas your child is naturally gifted in?

Explore the possibilities.

Just because three generations of your family have ended up as doctors doesn't mean that your child will too. Every child has a unique bent that will begin to reveal itself. You can't turn it in the direction you'd like it to go. Well, you can

47

try, but both you and your child will be unhappy in the long term. Instead, your job as parent is to understand what that bent is, find ways to naturally incorporate it in your home as your child grows, and explore the possibilities of using it in a future career through educational options suited to your child.

Let's say your son seems to be mechanically minded. From babyhood he spent hours stacking and restacking blocks. Then he graduated to building forts with Lincoln logs and skyscrapers with Legos. He loves to do puzzles and even took apart an old camera to see how it worked. You likely have an engineer or architect in the works. Exploring how buildings are put together—through drawings, the materials used, etc.—would be a fascinating journey to take with your son. If your basement is unfinished, why not involve your son in helping to construct a wall? You may not be handy, but perhaps your neighbor is. And he may appreciate your barbecuing talents as a swap for his construction skills.

Maybe your daughter enjoys playing numbers games and seems to have a penchant for mathematics. You might have a master's in accounting yourself. But if you're working on your family budget, why not say to your 11-year-old, "Honey, I could really use your help on this, if you're interested." Then invent some math problems your child can work on that could be plugged into your budget. Doing so will show your child how math is used in the real world.

Or perhaps your young son has always loved drawing. You find his doodles on the corners of books and on the wall in his closet. If you have a blank wall in your laundry room that could use some artwork, why not encourage his talents? You might be surprised what he'll come up with. And even if it isn't worthy of an art gallery at the moment, I can guarantee you'll look at it 10 years from now and smile. While you're at it, why not take your son to an art gallery or enroll him in a summer art class?

The best way to find your child's bent is to explore options in a fun, natural way. Even better if, in exploring the options, your child can create something that contributes to your family and home.

Keep the options broad.

In our parental drive to help our kids excel, it's easy to push them too hard. Yes, your child may have talents in gymnastics, but if you focus on that one area and she doesn't make the gymnastics team in high school, what other interests will she have developed along the way? That one failure will hit hard if gymnastics has been her sole focus.

When your children are young, it's important to keep their options of activities broad. Instead of zeroing in on one particular area of strength, allow them to try out different interests. However, let me be blunt. Trying out different interests doesn't mean that you and your child do them all simultaneously. You're human beings, not gerbils running mindlessly on a never-ending activity wheel.

> When your children are young, it's important to keep their options of activities broad. Instead of zeroing in on one particular area of strength, allow them to try out different interests.

49

In the Leman family, we had an ironclad rule—one activity per kid per semester. Never more. Why? We wanted our kids to have time to be kids. Every child needs playtime and the space to dream. We also believed that no one member of the family was more important than the family as a whole. We Lemans were all pieces of one pie. Everybody's opinion mattered. We wanted to eat together, work together, and play together. If we were all running different directions, we'd never intersect. It was enough to juggle five activities a week—one for each child.

And finally, we wanted to create children who weren't "all about me" but learned what it was like to meet others' needs with love and compassion. So as a family we did many activities that would grow our children's hearts. We gave of our time and talents to bring joy to elderly residents, extended money to homeless urban citizens, invited lonely individuals to come on our family outings, and delivered groceries to people in need. For Sande and me, education isn't just about what you learn in your head; it's about stretching your heart to include others.

Engage their natural curiosity.

Every child is born naturally curious and ready to explore the world within their reach. For babies, that's their toes. For toddlers, it's anything they can find to put in their mouth. Today's preschoolers and kindergarteners are often already tech savvy, thanks to smartphones and internet games, but are more socially curious as their immediate world expands beyond parents, siblings, and grandparents. Every good school has to connect with a child's natural curiosity and encourage an inquisitive mind.

For example, your sixth grader asks you a question based on a national event she heard about at school.

"Honey, that's a great question," you say. "Truth is, I don't know. But let's google it right now."

If your child is interested in something, continue the conversation. All it takes is a simple, "Tell me more about that."

When my grandson, Conner, was seven years old and I was speaking in Florida, I got a phone call from him. "Grandpa," he said, "watch out for the alligator gar fish."

I didn't have a clue what the alligator gar fish was and had to google it. But my grandson, who knows every sea creature that has ever existed because he has absorbed all his research like a sponge, was concerned because I was by the ocean. He knew that an alligator gar fish was big—five feet long—and could really hurt you. His compassionate heart didn't want his grandpa to get hurt, so he wanted to make sure I was on the lookout.

> Children have a natural desire for learning—if it's fun and not forced.

Kudos to my daughter Krissy for not only encouraging Conner's interests but also helping him develop the kind of heart that cares about others.

Children have a natural desire for learning—if it's fun and not forced. They want to know why, when, and where. Two-year-olds can drive you crazy with their constant "Why?" questions. They also have the keen instinct to ask when you don't have time to answer. But it's important never to shut down that curious nature. If you don't have time, simply say, "Honey, I'm really curious what brought on that thought. I can't talk more right now, but I want to pick up this conversation later." And when you don't know the answer, simply admit that. Have fun researching the topic together.

What's most important is that you encourage the interests of your child. A lot of kids struggle in math and science because they find them boring. That's one of the reasons we brought in a program called "Mad Science" at Leman Academy of Excellence. Fun people come in with white lab coats and do cool science experiments that would fascinate anybody not even vaguely interested in science. It's a lively, interactive program. If your child is interested in science, why not get him a magazine subscription? Take a field trip to the local forest preserve and investigate leaves and flowers. Or if your child is athletically oriented, explore clubs such as tae kwon do and gymnastics.

> You, parent, are the most active ingredient in your child's education menu.

In your child's lifelong education, he will need other teachers. But you, parent, are the most active ingredient in your child's education menu. All others—even the school your child might attend regularly—are a la carte items. They complement your teaching, which is the main dish for your child.

Keep expectations realistic, but set the bar high.

When your child shows an interest in something, keep your expectations realistic. If he's young, his interest may be very short-lived. If he's older, his interest may be more intensely driven. If you think the interest is a simple but passing curiosity, engage in a single event or activity.

For example, your 9-year-old daughter announces she wants to be an archaeologist because she saw one on a *National Geographic* TV special. You know of an interactive program at a museum in a city nearby, so you set aside a Saturday and go. Your daughter has the opportunity to dig for fossils with other children in a pit . . . and soon realizes that it's a lot of hard work. She spends more time socializing with the kids than actually digging for the fossils. Clearly she doesn't have the follow-through or personality to become a dedicated archaeologist. But you've both experienced something new, and she's satisfied that she got to check out her interest. And now there's no need to involve her in the semester-long program that would require you to drive to the museum every Saturday.

If the activity is one that your child seems more interested in and you think she might flourish at it, then agree that she'll do it for a short time at first—such as a summer, a quarter or semester of school, or a full school year. But set the bar high for your child to finish what she started.

"If you want to try helping out with the yearbook," you say, "I think it's great. But you'll need to do it for the whole school year. After that, if you want to continue, that's your call. If you don't, that's your call too."

In other words, you hold your child accountable to complete what she started. Don't let her off the hook when things are inconvenient and hard. But you also don't sentence her to a lifetime imprisonment just because she showed interest in something.

Ditto with your son, who wanted to run track for the season because his friends were going to, but then swiftly realized that it's a sweaty, exhausting venture.

There are occasions, though, where you need to break the rules. Kudos to a mom I know for doing so.

Katharine's firstborn daughter, Caryn, has phenomenal music talent. Caryn was greatly motivated at age 4 to learn how to play the violin after seeing a professional orchestra perform. Both mom and daughter plunged into an intense Suzuki program, and Caryn loved it. She continued the program outside of her regular school, since orchestra wasn't even offered there until middle school. But by the time Caryn was a sophomore in high school, she was finding excuses not to go to lessons. Strangely, though, she still spent hours playing violin in her free time.

> Hold your child accountable to complete what she started. Don't let her off the hook when things are inconvenient and hard.

Katharine knew it was time for a frank conversation. "Honey, I notice that you don't seem happy any longer at lessons. But I believe you're really talented at the violin, and you clearly still like to play, since you do it in your free time. I'd like to know what you're thinking and feeling about this. And I promise I will listen to every word you have to say. No one knows you better than you do."

That kind of statement told Caryn that her mother respected her thoughts and feelings, and it opened the door for her to talk freely about what she had struggled with for the past year. "Mom, I still love the violin, but I can't stand to play 'Twinkle, Twinkle, Little Star' one more time. I want more variety and the time to explore other kinds of music."

Caryn was bored with the standard curriculum and repetition of the Suzuki program. It was no longer a challenge, and she had exceeded the knowledge of her current teacher. (Frankly, as a baby of the family, I wouldn't have survived long in such a method! Caryn had been in the program more than 11 years.) She instead thrived on always having the carrot of new techniques out in front of her and had been experimenting with other genres of violin music. "I also want to create music on my own," she confessed.

So that mom and daughter, who are both hard-driving, finish-what-you-start people, broke their own rules. They met with Caryn's beloved violin teacher and explained what they were doing and why, and then Katharine officially removed her daughter from the program midsemester. They began watching concerts and YouTube clips of different styles of violin music together. As Caryn experimented, Katharine continued being an avid listener and encourager of her daughter's natural talents.

Now, a year later, Caryn—who has a rigorous academic schedule and is a straight-A student heading for a top university—has had the opportunity to happily explore musical genres, write her own music, and play in the pit orchestra of multiple musicals.

I applaud Katharine for breaking her own rules. If she was a hard-liner and not engaged relationally with her daughter, she could have said something like, "How could you want to quit lessons? Last year you got the Maestro Award at school. So how could you possibly say that?"

But with such words, she would have sparked an argument and then closed the door of her daughter's heart. Instead, Katharine chose to trust her smart, hardworking daughter's

> ## Four Top Qualities of Good Students
>
> - They naturally desire to learn.
> - They are curious, always asking why, how, and when.
> - They don't give up easily. If something doesn't work, they try another way.
> - They have parents who admit they don't know everything and look for answers with their children.

instinct and walk alongside her. Frankly, after 11 years, Caryn had earned the right to say she wanted to do something different.

You see, knowing your child's learning style, strengths and weaknesses, and natural bent can provide only part of your child's educational menu. What's most important is the relationship between you and your child. Sometimes knowing her talents means that you need to bend the rules to obtain the best education for her. That's when your parental discernment kicks in.

No one knows your child better than you. That's why you're the best person in the world to capitalize on your child's strengths and talents and provide opportunities to satisfy her natural curiosity.

3

Schooling a la Carte

Wading through the plethora of options—pros and cons.

When I was growing up in western New York, my parents didn't have a lot of choices in schooling options. There was the public school in our area and . . . the public school. My mom not only kept track of three kids—the troublesome one being me—but also worked as a nurse. Most of the time she had the nighttime shift. I can still remember getting out of bed in the morning, peering out the window into the falling snow, and seeing my mom walking home from work toward our house. I doubt she knew that homeschooling even existed, and she wouldn't have had the time or energy to pursue it.

But today there is a wide menu of options for parents to choose from, and they can even mix and match. What you choose for your child will have a lot to do with three corners of a triangle:

- your child's natural strengths, talents, learning styles, and personality
- the school's philosophies, teaching styles, and environment
- your background, expectations, and beliefs as a parent

Each corner of the triangle is a critical part of the overall picture of education. All are needed, no matter what schooling choices you make. Even homeschooling parents are involved with co-ops that include other teachers or mix and match with classes at local schools. No matter how fabulous a school is, it can never replace the parent end of the triangle. Yet due to so many fractured families today, many schools are asked to do both the teaching and other things traditionally performed by families, such as feeding children, providing before- and after-school care, and counseling troubled children. As a result, schools carry a heavier weight than they used to.

Exploring the Options

In this chapter, we'll cover the basics of a plethora of options you have to choose from in the schooling menu:

- charter schools
- home schools
- magnet schools
- military schools

- private schools (religious, parochial, or other)
- public schools
- virtual/online schools
- vocational schools

Charter schools

A charter school is an independently run public school of choice, which means parents can make the choice for their children, instead of simply sending them to the regular public school in their district.

Each charter school has specific missions, programs, performance goals, and methods they use to assess academic performance. Unlike regular public schools, if the charter school doesn't perform well and meet their charter goals—in terms of academic achievement and financial management—it may be closed.

Charter schools can be a single school (at one location or multiple locations), a grouping of schools that work together, or a network of schools or charter management organizations (CMOs), such as Uncommon Schools. CMOs are organizations that offer management services such as developing curriculum, recruiting teachers, locating or building facilities, and providing testing assessments. The focus is always on ensuring that individual students will achieve their fullest potential.

With a name like *charter school*, parents assume that tuition is involved. However, a charter school is a state school, not a private school, so it's tuition free but with specialized education. It can emphasize sports, music, science, math, the classics, the arts, or something else. The advantage of a charter school is that it starts from scratch with teaching and learning philosophies and with hiring faculty and staff. It doesn't have tenured teachers who have taught for years, even if they are as boring as sticks and are only punching the clock. And the school can go after staff who do their administrative tasks well and are child friendly.

Classical charter schools are based on the trivium (a Latin word meaning "where three roads meet"), a three-stage approach to education—grammar, logic, and rhetoric. For example, a classical charter school such as Leman Academy of Excellence includes studying Latin and different time periods. All learning is coordinated and interrelated. If sixth graders are studying Germany during the time period of World War II, they might read *The Diary of Anne Frank*; study a German philosopher, artist, or conductor; and learn about German food and geography—all part of one integrated theme. Sending your child to a very good charter school is like sending your child to a private school for free.

> **With a name like *charter school*, parents assume that tuition is involved. However, a charter school is a state school, not a private school, so it's tuition free but with specialized education.**

Charter schools and private schools have a better shot at creating a social environment that's conducive to learning since they start from scratch to build their philosophies and the environment. Because they can build faculty brick by brick, they have a higher probability of bringing in teachers who want to be in the classroom and who appreciate the new environment the school is going to create. They're also flexible in attending to the needs of children and respect and applaud individuality and diversity. Charter schools tend to attract parents who are serious about education and fed up with typical public school education. They may be disappointed with administrative procedures, the lack of rules or the rules within a specific school, the caustic environment within the student body, or the bullying and fighting. Many parents see charter schools as a fresh start and an opportunity to allow their child to receive a broad but specialized education that will prepare them for life after school.

But look carefully before you jump into one. Not every charter school is created equal. They are as different as zebras are from centipedes. Some survive and some don't. Charter schools stay afloat financially more than some private schools because the state pays a preset dollar amount per year (depending on the particular state) for educating each child sitting in a seat. Bottom line: a charter school is a business. That school has to pay the bills, so it needs administrators who are prudent and able to stay within budgets, instead of getting carried away with the once-a-year windfall from the state. Good charter schools make sure they watch the business end carefully and also hire teachers who truly love kids and have a passion for teaching outside the normal grid.

Home schools

Homeschooling is education of children at home by their parents or a chosen tutor. It can be used as a primary means of education or a form of supplemental education.

The homeschooling movement is growing in huge numbers for a variety of reasons. One is dissatisfaction with the available local schools due to the environment (morals, bullying, etc.), the academic instruction, the type of curriculum, and the way the school deals with a child's individual needs. Another reason is the parents' desire to be more integrally involved in their child's education, including having greater control over how their child is taught, the ability to cater to specific strengths and weaknesses, and the drive to provide targeted education that matches a family's worldview.

If you're in a small town that's known for poor-quality schools, or in a rural area where the closest school is quite a drive, what do you do? For some, homeschooling is a necessity. Not only do you get to educate your son or daughter, but you also have the opportunity to reeducate yourself. If you don't have a teaching degree, you're treading in unknown waters.

> **The homeschooling movement is growing in huge numbers for a variety of reasons.**

Some families choose homeschooling because they believe in the importance of the family setting and nonacademic learning, such as hands-on internships and the ability to focus broadly or specifically on subjects a child may be interested in. Some families travel frequently due to a parent's job, and homeschooling can provide ongoing stability in a child's education. Young athletes, actors, and musicians are also homeschooled in order to accommodate the intensity of their schedules and training. Other children are homeschooled because the parents highly believe in mentorship and life internships—where one or more committed individuals can walk alongside a child in learning a particular craft.

Professional educators tend to hold polar-opposite views of homeschooled children. Some say they can tell who the homeschooled kids are because they are so smart, targeted, and ahead of the curve. Others say that homeschooled children are ill-prepared not only for rigorous academics but also for social interactions, and thus struggle later in life. The difference, I'm convinced, has everything to do with the parents:

- their abilities—organizational strengths, broad knowledge, and willingness to learn what they don't know
- their resourcefulness—persistence in researching what they don't know and making the proper connections
- their personality—patience and determination to power through hurdles
- their parenting style—the ability to separate home and school and to provide the right authoritative balance between pushing and encouraging a child academically and in areas of interest

Parents in the trenches of homeschooling can provide even more necessary qualities than these, so why not dialogue with a few of them and do some more reading if this is an area of interest for you?

As we discussed schooling options for our kids, I once brought up homeschooling to my wife.

"What?" she said, baring her teeth like a German shepherd patrolling the junkyard against potential adversaries.

That was the end of the subject for us. With such an expression on my normally sweet Sandra's face, I didn't have

63

the courage to bring it up again. Sande knew instinctively that she functioned best as mom and natural educator of life along the way, but not as a homeschooling teacher.

Parents who homeschool admit that they often struggle with their dual roles as mom or dad and teacher, and sometimes it's difficult to separate the two. Being your child's teacher is a little like teaching your spouse how to drive. It's possible but tricky.

Also, there are some practical drawbacks. When a kid misbehaves, where do you send him if you're both parent and teacher? To the backyard? This is why homeschooling is sometimes a tough road to walk, but it can be accomplished if there are set boundaries between schooltime, family time, and playtime, and the personalities of parent and child are a good match. Those who find that happy balance in homeschooling long-term say that having a room or space in the house dedicated to homeschooling and keeping certain hours are important for establishing those boundaries.

You all walk through the door at 8:00 a.m., have a short recess during the morning, and have a lunch break, and then school is done by 1:00 or 1:30. You close the door to the schoolroom and don't enter it as teacher until the next day. During class hours—whether in the classroom, on a field trip, or driving to a co-op—you are the teacher. Before and after those hours you are the parent.

Recently I was honored to be part of a focus group with homeschooling parents. I wanted to know what was on their minds the most. The biggest question they all had was about curriculum. "Do I buy a single box curriculum, or do I go with the piecemeal approach?"

Many had decided to go with the latter, especially if they were homeschooling multiple children. One woman taught five children, and their skills in math and science were all over the place. So if you have one child who is strong in math and another who struggles with 2 + 2, then you may need different curriculums. Interestingly, many of them mentioned that Rainbow Resource Center had been helpful to them in choosing curriculum that would fit their individual children.

Also, though parents chose this method of education because they wanted a piece of the action—to be a teacher to their child—many had chosen to complement it with other educational options. For example, a child might be homeschooled three days a week and then spend two days on campus at a charter school nearby. Or a child might be homeschooled every day and then go to a private school or community program for a couple of classes a week, such as music, art, or PE.

Co-ops were very important to most of the homeschooling parents. The strength of the co-op, they said, is that it creates a classroom atmosphere. Also, if one parent wasn't passionate about science but another was, their children could be combined into a class to take full advantage of the parent who was strong in science. That option benefitted both parents and students. Parents faced less work in handling multiple subjects and were more comfortable dealing with areas where they were experts, and students had the benefit of teachers who loved their subject.

Intriguingly, all the parents agreed that homeschooling must be done in the morning. Even if they had a wide range of age differences in their children, none of the parents saw any benefit in starting later. When they tried starting at 10:00

instead of 8:00 to benefit late risers, they ended up killing time, and then by 10:00 the children who had been up for a while had more difficulty engaging. Children function better if they have an earlier start to their school day. Ditto for the parent as teacher. If you run errands or do housework before school, by the time you're ready to start, you've lost your motivation and enthusiasm.

That meeting with the homeschooling parents was invigorating, because they were so passionate about playing a part in their child's education. And they were also very flexible in talking about wonderful a la carte items and desserts on the education menu.

For those of you who choose to homeschool, it is an awesome commitment to be in charge of educating your child. After all, no one knows your child better than you. And there's a lot of curriculum available to choose from, or to mix and match, to ensure your child is getting good grade-level instruction and enrichment.

The a la carte options for homeschooling, combined with other educational avenues, are abundant. Many children who are schooled at home do attend classes elsewhere. Some attend teaching co-ops, where a parent certified in math might teach that subject for the entire homeschooling group. Physical education experiences could come from local or community classes, such as karate or badminton, or through soccer or baseball leagues. Other homeschoolers supplement with classes at local charter schools, such as Veritas. These arrangements also allow homeschooled children a place to gather socially for a few hours a week. Some homeschoolers join private schools for a couple of hours a day or week for specific classes, such as a science lab. With today's global connections, a homeschooler can take nearly any subject through a virtual or online academy. Your child could live in Nebraska but take Japanese with a first-generation speaker through an online language school.

If you are interested in the homeschooling route, you may want to read books by Susan Sutherland Isaacs, Charlotte Mason, or John Holt for some background on the philosophies behind homeschooling. Or attend a local homeschooling event or conference to meet parents in the trenches and get an overview of the curriculum available. Many parents of the Christian faith are very comfortable with the A Beka Academy online curriculum. It provides "excellence in education from a Christian perspective"[1] and covers grades K–12 with challenging college-prep education, with the advantage that the parent does not have to be a professional teacher. They also support parents with events, meetings, and conferences.

Whether you decide to homeschool or not, it's important to take charge of your child's education—to be active in it.

Magnet schools

A magnet school is a public school and therefore free, but it offers programs and instruction that are designed to attract a diverse student body. It's an upper-end school for competent, focused, serious students.

Magnet schools may have different connotations in different areas of the country. A student can live 10 miles outside the public school district where the magnet school is and still attend the school. Magnet schools focus on a theme and align their curriculum accordingly in a variety of areas, such as fine and performing arts; career and technical education;

international studies; world languages; and science, technology, engineering, and mathematics (STEM). They use more hands-on learning that is based on discovery and performances or projects. Because they are public schools, they still use the state's standard curriculum in all subject areas. But the subjects are taught from the framework of the overall theme of the school.

> A magnet school is a public school and therefore free, but it offers programs and instruction that are designed to attract a diverse student body. It's an upper-end school for competent, focused, serious students.

The only eligibility needed to attend a magnet school is a student's interest in its theme. For example, your child is interested in fine arts and is showing a proclivity for it. Or he has an ear for languages. Or perhaps he lights up every time he is able to increase his scientific knowledge.

Though all magnet schools consider diversity a critical element and thus have a wide variety of students, some magnet schools are slanted more for extremely talented and gifted children. Those schools will assess the skills of specific students and also look at teacher or parent recommendations in order to select their students. Such magnet schools have high expectations. Most of the kids who go there really want to be there and are the kinds of serious students who end up taking AP classes. Magnet schools tend to attract children who are advanced, have thought life through, and have a good handle already on their pluses and minuses and what skills they could bring to a future job situation. In other words, they are *intentional* children, already knowing where they are headed.

Magnet schools are for those who

- value diversity in the student population
- aren't concerned about peers being from similar socio-economic or cultural backgrounds or having a shared belief system
- are committed, serious students who have already fine-tuned their life direction
- have interest in particular areas of education and a specialized teaching staff
- enjoy interacting with others who have similar interests in a highly social environment (magnet schools are big on community and cultivating school spirit)
- have parents who value being engaged in their child's learning process

Some students who show talent in a particular area might spend their last year or two of high school in a magnet school to develop their skills. Because students at these schools have shared interests, they tend to have a wide social network, good academics, fewer discipline problems, personalized learning because class numbers are smaller than those in public schools, and a sense of community that extends to their family. Also, because these kids are high achievers and have broad interests—though they may be particularly skilled in one area—it wouldn't be unusual for a student to be an egghead, play in the local symphony orchestra, be on the chess team, play on a tennis league, and also be able to make a clarinet do everything but a push-up.

WHAT WE DID

When Nick was 12, his childhood friends became very involved with basketball and soccer. He became fascinated with making pottery. My ex, who thought art was for girls, pushed my son toward becoming an industrial engineer. He also wanted him to "toughen up," so he signed Nick up for a soccer league "to get art out of his system." Nick played soccer that summer because he didn't want to go against his dad, but he hated every minute of it.

The kid I knew had always loved to work with his hands. When he was young, one of his favorite activities was shaping sculptures with Play-Doh. Then he discovered textured paint, and his bedroom walls became his canvas, which also drove my ex crazy.

The next summer, Nick asked if he could do a class at the local pottery shop. We talked together to the owner, and it seemed like a great fit.

"That was the best summer I can remember," Nick told me recently. "Thanks for fighting for what was important to me."

That summer sparked our brainstorm to change his schooling. Nick had been attending a school that was big on the four basics—math, science, history, English—but had cut art out of the curriculum due to funding. We discussed adding some community art classes after school and on weekends, but then realized that with me working full-time and him working an after-school job to help us make ends meet, there was no time for night and weekend hours in another activity. So we made a big leap. We transferred him to a magnet school that emphasized art, even though it was a little farther away from our home. There Nick found a network of friends who loved and explored all kinds of art forms, just like he did.

Nick graduated from university with an art degree and began teaching full-time at an art academy. I will always be glad that I fought hard for what was important to my son, even when it was tough.

Last month I had the honor of being his guest at his first gallery show in California. As I looked at the pottery and paintings, I thought of all the times in his childhood when he'd chalked drawings on our driveway, made Play-Doh sculptures, and painted his walls. I know my son is doing exactly what he should be doing, and that makes me smile.

Military schools

Military school is also known as military academy or service academy. It's a targeted educational institution that trains young men and women for military careers. It seeks to prepare young people for service in the US military—Army, Navy, Air Force, Coast Guard, or Marine Corps.

Military schools are most often boarding schools that focus on educating boys and/or girls in grades 6–12, 7–12, 8–12, or 9–12. Many military schools are privately owned (see also "Private schools" below) and tuition based, though they also may offer scholarships. They are dedicated to helping young people develop leadership skills in an achievement-oriented, structured environment. Children learn how to take ownership of their own lives and develop what they need to be successful personally and professionally in their later years.

Because military schools are usually boarding schools, there are limited distractions to learning. The academic environment is usually quite challenging, and teachers also encourage the development of personal qualities, such as confidence, respect, service to others, and high moral character. The number of students in a class is smaller, so faculty are able to focus more on individual personalities, strengths, and challenges and to tailor programs to each child in addition to using the regular curriculum. Another advantage is that children live together, support each other, and learn from each other—thus forging positive, quality relationships that tend to last through their adult years.

> Military schools are dedicated to helping young people develop leadership skills in an achievement-oriented, structured environment.

Children who need structure and focus and who are easily distracted may benefit from military schooling. Aaron, for example, struggled all throughout elementary and middle school to focus on his studies and needed a lot of structure, interaction, and follow-up with his teachers to accomplish his tasks. He attended a school without a lot of structure, where rules were bent often and the administration backed parents and "popular" students over teachers, so teacher turnover was high. As a result, Aaron was given free rein. He was a likable kid who attracted others to him because of his looks, physical prowess, and leadership skills. When he got in trouble, though, so did his whole group of friends . . . and anyone else in the vicinity.

Besides football and basketball, he ran track and joined the wrestling team to wear off some of his excess energy, but it wasn't enough to keep him out of trouble. His sophomore year of high school, he and his parents agreed he needed a school with more structure that worked better with his high-energy level and natural athletic abilities.

Military school was a great match for Aaron. He thrived in that environment. His social skills and giving spirit swiftly gained him a strong friendship network in the dorms because he was someone others could count on. The emphasis on physical education and strength training was a great match for his innate skills. His growing responsibilities thrust him into positions where he learned what excellence, character, and leadership are all about, and he decided he wanted a piece of the action.

Today Aaron is in his early twenties, confident, focused, undergoing training for Special Ops, and planning for a career in the military. He's at the top of his game in all ways. That result isn't surprising. Graduates of military schools usually develop confidence, integrity, and respect for others. They not only are willing to do whatever is needed to be the best they can be as individuals but are committed to teamwork and giving back to their community and our nation.

Private schools (religious, parochial, or other)

A private school is a school that is supported by a private organization or a group of private individuals rather than by local, state, or national fees, as public or charter schools are. Attending a private school of any kind means paying fees. The amount of fees depends on the school. Because government sources don't pay for the schooling, private schools have a right to select their students, who are funded in whole or in part by tuition fees paid by their parents or guardians. Some private schools receive funding from wealthy individuals or

73

groups who partially fund tuition for students. Some also offer scholarships or work programs, which can make the cost cheaper.

There are lots of types of private schools. They can be religiously affiliated (Catholic, Hebrew, Christian, Muslim) or denominational (Baptist, Lutheran, LDS, Orthodox). Some of the schools teach faith-based education along with the regular academic subjects, with the goal of impressing particular religious beliefs on the students. Others teach their denomination's beliefs but also cover academic subjects from all angles, maintaining a fine distinction between academics and religion.

A private school is a school that is supported by a private organization or a group of private individuals rather than by local, state, or national fees.

There are private all-boy schools, all-girl schools, and co-ed schools. Private schools can refuse admittance to those who don't measure up to their standards. They usually have smaller class sizes, and many have accelerated curriculum—most private schools tout rigorous curriculum that goes beyond a regular classroom. They may have extra features, such as high-class libraries from wealthy donors, science labs, and the latest technology. Also, discipline is more regulated and built into the system through school handbooks distributed to incoming students and their parents.

Private schools are usually pricey but can vary greatly on cost. Many parents are affluent or have relatives—particularly Grandma and Grandpa—who help with tuition and other fees. Parents who are interested in their children rubbing shoulders with kids of a similar socioeconomic level, who want advanced curriculum that may help their child get into prestigious universities, or whose belief structures are very important to them are attracted to these schools.

With faith-based schools, some parents may erroneously think that by sending their child there, they can cloister him from the real world—away from the "bad public school kids," as parents have told me time and time again. Reality is, even in a faith-based school, not every parent and child will think and act the way you want your child to think and act. Just because all participants signed a statement of faith doesn't mean they actually believe or live that statement.

Another erroneous conclusion is that if your child is taught the basics of your faith at school, then you don't have to worry about teaching them at home. You can check that "to do" off your list. However, if you are sending your child to a private school because you want a faith-based education to walk hand in hand with values you role-model at home, so your child is taught subjects within your context of faith and builds a strong moral foundation that won't waver, that's a different and admirable motive. School is not, and never should be, a replacement for teaching values and beliefs in your home.

Private schools, unless they have been established for a long time, can come and go swiftly due to funding issues. Some church schools are more mom-and-pop–type operations, with a limited number of students and teachers who may not be fully accredited. For example, a PE teacher may be called upon to teach Bible classes simply because he's taught Bible studies before and no one else is stepping up to the plate. These schools also, by their nature, don't usually have the resources to cater to special needs students or to tailor their programs to provide other helps students may need.

When checking out private schools, look at their longevity, teacher accreditations, curriculum, and fee structure to see if they match what you're looking for.

Public schools

A public school is a tuition-free school operated by the local, state, and national governments and funded by citizens' taxes. It includes primary and secondary schools.

The public school is usually very accessible—it's close by and easy to get to, and kids are regularly bused from their homes to school. Chances are that it also has a well-staffed special education department that is used to dealing with IEPs (Individualized Education Plans) and 504s—labels the school system uses to classify individuals who need specific help with learning. This department is likely better developed than that of most private schools. They have more people on staff to handle non-visual learners, reluctant readers, and those with physical disabilities. The programs have been established for years and so have a lot of kinks worked out of them.

> A public school is a tuition-free school operated by the local, state, and national governments and funded by citizens' taxes. It includes primary and secondary schools.

Many public schools use the Common Core curriculum, formed by governors in conjunction with educators in the state so there is a way of measuring children's learning. The term has become a political football that gets lobbed back and forth. Most parents wince when they hear it now.

The public school today is bashed regularly due to these issues, among others:

- the mentality that everyone has to be a winner
- overemphasis on political correctness
- the lack of discipline for students
- the lack of support for teachers by administration
- deplorable behavior of students that has become acceptable

In public schools today, teachers often report that their hands are tied. They are thrown like balsa wood on the ocean and tossed around with tremendous lack of respect by kids who are 12 to 14 years of age. They are F-bombed on a regular basis.

Kids can read the winds very well. If they know teachers aren't backed by administration, they know they can get away with behaviors they couldn't get away with anywhere else, including in their own home. I've often seen articles in my own hometown's paper about teachers who are being abused and struck by students. But much of the behavior starts with what the kids haven't learned at home—the basics of courtesy and respect. A teacher who has taught for over 30 years recently told me about a kindergartener who called her "a buttface" and said she was going to smack her in the mouth. That certainly tells me something about that child's home life.

But I want to be clear. There are some public schools and public school districts that are wonderful. They tend to have attitudes that are more in line with those of private and charter schools.

I know of a great public school district in the Tucson area. It all starts at the top with a well-educated and time-tested superintendent who takes his job seriously. Balanced discipline where children are held accountable is a regular part of the classroom, and expectations for academics and behavior are high. Each fall I give a talk there at the beginning of the school year, and the school invites all church and community organizations to attend, encouraging them to bring their materials and to be part of the school community. Yes, it's a public school, and technically separation of church and state still reigns in public schools. But why wouldn't that wise superintendent want to partner with groups in the community? Doing so makes for a better school and a better community.

So before you lump all public schools into one category, fueled by media reports of their failures, check out your local public school. Form your own unbiased conclusions of that particular one.

Virtual/online schools

A virtual or online school provides internet resources—lessons, teaching, homework—and operates primarily through those methods. They usually offer individual classes for students and parents who want a la carte options. Students and teachers may interact through email or face-to-face on the computer, or they may not interact at all, depending on the program. Virtual schools can cover grades K–12. Because of the progression of technology, the way that virtual/online schools work changes continually.

78

Virtual schools can have public, private, or homeschooling options. If public, they are governed by the same regulations as brick-and-mortar public schools where children sit in the classrooms, and they're free. State-certified teachers are still responsible to oversee and manage the learning of students and to assess and test them. Students take the same tests as those who are in the physical classroom, and curriculum is established. Any student may enroll. Those who have special education needs are also identified, and specialized school staff meet with them and their parent or guardian for evaluation.

> A virtual or online school provides internet resources—lessons, teaching, homework—and operates primarily through those methods.

Many private and charter schools now also offer online classes to students who couldn't otherwise attend by setting up video cameras in the classroom and posting lessons online.

If your child is educated partly or mainly through an online school, that doesn't automatically mean that they're homeschooled. The parent doesn't have to find or choose the curriculum—it's already chosen, whether it's material from a public school, private school, or home school. However, the parent does need to work closely with their child, guiding them through daily lessons or at least spot-checking when a lesson is complete.

Curriculums such as Veritas and A Beka are based on a Christian education and offer virtual schooling. Connections Academy also offers homeroom teacher and online classes. They have dedicated tutors and lecturers who provide children with a variety of subjects from teachers with diverse backgrounds and experiences.

Virtual/online schools offer myriad options as a primary method of learning or as a la carte classes.

If you are interested in faith-based learning and options that might not be offered at your public school or private school, academies such as Sevenstar offer all kinds of classes. One student I know attended a private school that only offered Spanish and French for foreign languages, but she wanted to take Chinese. She took it through Sevenstar, and the credits transferred directly to her private high school and were listed on her transcript for college. Another high schooler was intrigued by forensic science and took a class on that through Sevenstar.

Let me be blunt. If you have a highly active child who needs a lot of social interaction or guidance, having him sit in front of a computer screen for a major portion of his day isn't the best option. Virtual/online schooling works well with self-motivated children who can focus on a subject for a period of time by themselves without supervision.

Vocational schools

Vocational schools, sometimes called trade schools, prepare high school students with practical education and training for specific jobs or careers. (They're different from career colleges, which are post-secondary, for-profit education options and may run from one to two years.) They typically offer focused programs that swiftly pave the way to the workforce after graduation rather than focusing on academic training for scholars who are pursuing professional careers. However, some vocational schools not only train their students technically but also include academics.

These schools are usually government owned or at least government supported and typically extend for two years rather than four. Credits received at vocational schools are usually transferrable to academic colleges.

Schools can teach all the academics they want. However, if they don't have a way to apply that learning by putting kids in the trenches and giving them a dose of what it's like to pursue specific careers in the real world, the education isn't a complete venture.

A friend of mine was hired several years ago by a college to teach an in-the-trenches journalism class after the college received numerous complaints from companies who had hired their graduates. The complaints basically claimed, "The graduates are well educated and smart. But they have no idea how to tailor their writing to an audience. They only want to write what they want to write."

> **Vocational schools, sometimes called trade schools, prepare high school students with practical education and training for specific jobs or careers.**

Vocational schools allow children to explore specific careers hands-on, especially those in the skilled trades. They are literally internships that allow students to experience what it's like to do a particular job before they become entrenched in it.

Vocational schools are good options for students who love to work with their hands or have strong inclinations toward the skilled trades. They are also smart choices for students who aren't academically oriented but could fly when given the opportunity to do what they love—whether in auto mechanics, culinary arts, forestry, farming, or firefighting.

Choosing from the Large Menu

Now that your head is swimming from the large number of choices on the education menu, it's time to step back and take a breath before you evaluate your options.

Your primary role with your child is to be their parent. That means providing learning experiences but not dictating, encouraging them to jump over hurdles but not forcing them to confront bars that are so high they're discouraging.

Among all the details, what's most important is that the schooling options fit your specific child. That's where the rubber meets the road.

Let's say you have a child who is over-the-top interested in athletics. He can tell you every major league baseball player of significance. He knows every football and basketball team backward and forward. He lives, breathes, and plays sports of all kinds, including soccer. You just found out that starting up in your area is a charter school that emphasizes sports. That would be a good place for you to investigate. However, charter schools are usually smaller, which means less competition for him athletically. That could be good or bad, based on your child's temperament. It would also be helpful for you to investigate the local public school, since public schools usually have a full array of sports available.

Or let's say you have a child who lives and breathes music. She's in a private school that has a so-so music department and no specialized music classes, though the school is great academically. She might be a great match for the fine arts magnet school that's across town and puts on five-star performances and plays.

It all comes down to your relationship to your child. How well do you know your real child versus your ideal child?

Your real child is who your child is now—her talents and abilities. Your ideal child is who you are projecting her to be—your desires for her in the future, who you'd like her to become, the gifts you'd like her to develop. Yes, your child may fulfill some of those thoughts and dreams, but only if they are also hers—not just yours.

Realistically, in what kind of school environment will your kid thrive?

What has worked at one time in your child's life may not work long-term. You need to be flexible and realistic about the fact that options may need to change.

Your son, who is highly involved in sports, may want to move from the faith-based school he likes, which doesn't have a football team, to the local public high school that has an award-winning football team.

Your daughter, who currently attends a charter school and is thriving there, may decide she wants to pursue through an online class a foreign language not available at her school. So the two of you decide that she'll move to a partial home-schooling schedule for her first class period so she can take specialized studies in language.

It's all about balance. Yes, you do need a schooling plan. But those plans don't have to be rigid, with no room for movement as your child's needs change. What should always be on your educational menu is what's best for your child.

4

Finding Just the Right Menu for Your Palate

Selecting the perfect education options to bring out the best in your child.

It's the first day of school. Ms. Adams, the first-grade teacher, greets one of her new little scholars, Adriana, with a smile. "It's so nice to meet you," she says. "Your last name is Sutherland, right?"

Adriana nods.

"Any chance you're related to James?" Ms. Adams asks.

Adriana looks down and shuffles her feet. Her red backpack hangs off one shoulder. One of her shoelaces is askew. "Yes," she finally says. "He's my brother."

Ms. Adams happily claps her hands. "Well then, you and I are going to have a great year!"

Last year Ms. Adams had James Sutherland in her class. If there was ever a teacher's pet, he was it—always first in line to help, a great kid who loved learning, a class leader, clearly liked by everyone, kind to others.

Well, time-out, teacher. You really don't know who you have sitting in aisle 4, seat 3. Her last name is Sutherland and her first name is Adriana, but you might as well call her Attila the Hun, because she is going to rock your world in a way that will shock even a seasoned teacher to the core.

Ms. Adams assumed that just because Adriana is James's sister, their experience in school will be the same. No, it won't. In fact, since older brother is so perfect in everyone's eyes, little sister will go out of her way to run in the opposite direction.

Besides getting a history lesson about Attila the Hun in twenty-first-century form, that teacher will feel like Custer making a last stand with the new little Sutherland, likely by the end of the first week.

Your Kids Are Created Equal but Not the Same

Parents make the same mistake as Ms. Adams did all the time. They assume that because their kids are all siblings, they'll act the same. However, the firstborn child is the lab rat of the family. Both parents experiment with him, so no wonder he focuses on trying to be perfect all the time. Then comes child number 2, who looks at child number 1. When the benchmark for worth is that perfect firstborn, how can the next child compete? So what does she do? She screams through her behavior, "Hello! I am not my brother, I'm me. Would someone please take the time to notice I'm me? I'm a different person."

Parent, do you treat your children differently? Trying to treat them the same is a recipe for disaster. Your children should have different bedtimes and different allowances based on their ages and needs. They should receive birthday gifts suited especially and solely for them. If you gave all three of your kids a skateboard for Christmas, one would be thrilled and head out the door to try it out, another would look at you like you're crazy, and the third might cry. Better gifts might be a season pass to the museum for your history buff and an iTunes gift card for your indie music lover. Your kids are created equal and are all important members of your household, but they are not the same. They clearly don't have the same learning styles or bents.

Why, then, would you pursue the same schooling options for all of them? Why not suit your educational approach to the uniqueness of each child?

By now your jaw has dropped. *Leman, are you nuts?* you're thinking. *I barely have enough time to brush my teeth and eat half an English muffin in the morning before I head out the door. I drink half of yesterday's cold coffee in the car on the way to work—one and a half hours on the expressway, by the way. And now you want me to run my kids to differ-ent schools? Maybe* you *ought to see a shrink.*

Granted, having your kids in more than one school is complicated and tough, for very practical reasons. But if your kids are spaced out in age, you may have them in different schools anyway—one in elementary, one in middle school, one in high school.

What I'm saying is that kids are diverse in their needs, makeup, and tastes. Perhaps your oldest loves macaroni and cheese, your middleborn hates it and refuses to eat it, and

WHAT WE DID

We have three boys—Mark, Andrew, and Jon—spaced two years apart. My wife and I felt strongly that homeschooling was the best option for our sons, based on our beliefs and the area where we live.

When our second son, Andrew, turned 13, we realized how much he loved sports. The homeschooling group we were involved with had always provided plenty of social interaction, but not much in the way of sports. Andrew really wanted to play football. He also told us he wanted more opportunities for friends than he currently had. After reading your *Birth Order Book*, we realized how important peer friendships are, but we were a little nervous about him attending the much larger local school. After debating it for a couple of years, we finally made the move last year, and we know we did the right thing.

Andrew's now at the public high school and a first-string player. He's also taken up wrestling and loves it. And he's known school-wide for his kindness and fairness to others, but no one messes with him because he stands firm on what he believes to be right. His relationship with his brothers has improved too, because he has time away from them. All three of them have learned to respect each other more for their unique abilities.

your youngest treats it as creative art when he tosses it from his high chair to decorate your kitchen wall. In the same way, a single item on the schooling menu won't work for all of them. Yes, you can try to make it work, but that isn't what's best for your kids.

So what will you choose? Convenience for yourself? Or the right schooling options for your children that will set them up for lifetime success?

I have five kids and four grandkids. It's amazing to me how fast the time flew that our kids were at home. It really does feel like the blink of an eye. Sande and I had many lean years financially because we decided early on, with our first child, that since my job involves a lot of travel, she would be the consistent parent always home for our kids. That meant, for her, setting aside dreams of owning her own eclectic shop (which she had later, when the kids were older). It also meant, for me, saying no to a lot of speaking engagements that overlapped with my children's activities and intruded on my time with them at home.

Our five kids are day-and-night different from each other, and we treated them as such. As we identified their bents and interests, we helped them pursue those through research, opportunities, activities, and educational options. None of them attended the same college or university, by the way. Today, each of them is passionate about their particular chosen careers.

- Holly, in school management and administration
- Krissy, in professional teacher development
- Kevin, in media entertainment
- Hannah, in marketing for a nonprofit
- Lauren, in art and design and as an entrepreneur

What worked for one child in our family didn't work for another child, because they weren't the same. Your children need a similar a la carte education service, with options perfectly suited to them, their learning styles, and their natural strengths.

Your Child's Unique Place in the Family

Another reason you should consider different schools for your kids is their birth order.

How many children do you have? Who was born first, second, and third? Wherever your child lands in the family line affects his life in countless ways, including the way that he learns. Just because you have three little cubs in your den doesn't mean they all respond the same to the same information. A large part of that has to do with their birth order.

Characteristics of different birth orders

Firstborns tend to be well organized and natural leaders. They're serious, scholarly, logical, and perfectionistic. They drive themselves and others hard. They're often extra tech savvy, are always reliable and conscientious, and are list makers. They don't like surprises or curveballs of any kind. They want to know what's expected of them, when, and why. They are highly motivated to win at all costs.

Only children are firstborns times 10. They have all the qualities of firstborns and more. By age 7 they act like little adults. They're high achievers and black-and-white thinkers, and they tend to talk in extremes ("You always . . . ," "I never . . ."). Failure is not an option to them. They have very high expectations of themselves. They're less comfortable with their peers than with older people. After all, they grew up with two parents whose eagle eyes were on them. As a result, they are very deliberate and thorough in all they do. They tend to be fearful and cautious. Whereas firstborns are voracious readers, onlies are unstoppable readers. Books are their best friends.

Middleborns will always go in the exact opposite direction of the firstborn. They're too smart to try to compete with the firstborn star of the family. That star is the trailblazer, so the middleborn decides, *Hey, I'm going to do something completely different.* Because middleborns are stuck in the middle, they grow admirable skills in mediation since they frequently play that role with their siblings. They are born diplomats who avoid conflict. Compromising is second nature to them since they haven't often won in any war with their firstborn sibling. With parental attention often focused on the firstborn star and the adventure-loving baby of the family, middleborns are used to not being in the limelight. So it's no surprise that they have many friends, are greatly loyal to them, and are good at keeping secrets.

Lastborns are natural entertainers who could talk with anyone. They are affectionate and charming and can wind anyone around their little finger if they try hard enough. Older siblings frequently send the babies to ask for parental favors because those favors are likely to be granted. As the cute ones of the family, they are most likely to retain their pet names. As lovers of attention, they attract others to them and are natural salespeople. They live for surprises and treat life as a party.

As you look at your kids, you may be thinking, *So why don't they fit that grid?* Birth order isn't as simple as just each child's place in the family line. Other factors come into play.

90

- If there is a five-year gap between children, the next child starts a new "family."
- If one of your children has physical or mental challenges, or a child dies, another child can usurp their role in the family.
- If your firstborn is a male and your secondborn is a female, both can act like firstborns, because they are the first of each sex.
- If one of your children is adopted, that can affect the birth order position, depending on how old the child was at adoption.
- If your family is a blended one, the birth order position of each child may change.
- If you are a critical-eyed, flaw-picking parent, that can upset the birth order apple cart big-time.

Still other factors include your parenting style, personality, and expectations, which will be discussed in the next chapter. For more specifics on variables in birth order and how it influences individuals and families, check out *The Birth Order Book*. You'll find fascinating information there about what makes your children tick and how to get the best out of them—and yourself too.

How birth order affects schooling options

How does birth order affect schooling options? It's simple. Do your kids all like to eat the same things? No? Then why would you offer them the same education menu and expect them all to like it?

Treating everyone equally isn't the best modus operandi for education. Every birth order has specific strengths and weaknesses.

Firstborns and onlies already have a lot of internal motivation to do everything perfectly. They don't need any further push because they already live with a lot of self-inflicted stress. The worst thing for a firstborn or only is criticism from a parent. The best thing you can do to lighten the pressure on them is to give them fewer responsibilities at home. Firstborns tend to take on too much, stacking the deck further against themselves by adding an enormous amount of activities to their rigorous schooling schedule. They can benefit from a parental look at their schedule options before they overload and exhaust themselves.

> **Treating everyone equally isn't the best modus operandi for education. Every birth order has specific strengths and weaknesses.**

Firstborns and onlies often thrive in high academic environments and like to work best by themselves. They can be annoyed by working in groups since others don't often jump as high as they do, nor are they as precise. Failure is not tolerated. However, they're also natural leaders who rise to the top when in group settings. Firstborns and onlies like to be in control and easily follow schedules. Home, charter, public, and magnet schools specific to their gifted areas, or virtual/online schools where they can work at their own pace, are particularly suited to firstborns and onlies. Still, because they tend to be lone rangers, they can benefit greatly from interaction in group activities, whether those are part of their regular school environment or extracurricular activities. No

---

What Can You Do for Your Firstborn or Only Child?

- Help streamline extra activities and responsibilities.
- Never criticize. Your child is hard enough on himself.
- Put mistakes and failures in their proper perspective.
- Encourage stress-free, regroup time.

---

matter the schooling environment, firstborns and onlies tend to rise to the top.

Middleborns thrive best in educational environments where they can be involved in a peer group with other non-family members. Also, schooling them differently than their older sibling can greatly be to their advantage, because then they don't have to work so hard to compete. They won't feel squeezed so much between their siblings and can more easily develop their own abilities. In a different setting, they can be themselves, not simply someone's younger brother or sister.

Middleborns need to know they have a special place. Their thoughts, opinions, and feelings matter and deserve to be heard. Because middleborns are loyal, they have the ability to develop an extensive friend network and to be at the core of it, holding everyone together. As such, they can become powerful forces for change in the world, and the right education can make all the difference in the direction they go.

The other thing that makes a huge difference to middleborns is your belief in them. Middleborns sometimes need to be challenged to do their best and to pursue their interests since their social network is often more important to them than academics. If you encourage them in their areas

What Can You Do for Your Middleborn?

- Identify her individual gifts and support her activities.
- Appreciate and highlight her unique role in the family.
- Encourage her to develop a strong network of friends who share common values.
- Work hard to stay connected relationally by making one-on-one time with your more naturally secretive middleborn.

of strength, however, they can fly. Some of the greatest entrepreneurs in the world are middleborns.

Lastborns thrive on fun and relationships. If school isn't fun, they want no part of it. They sometimes struggle with learning to read and being able to focus for long periods of time on a single subject. Babies often find it difficult to stay on task by themselves, as they are easily distracted. Individual study and virtual study programs aren't usually the best options for them. They need more direction and interaction. They also crave social time. If those basic needs aren't met, they won't find any meaning or purpose in pursuing academics. Lastborns need a reason to study.

They're also very good at getting others to do their work for them because they're so charming. After all, they've lived this far by manipulating their older siblings into rescuing them from consequences.

I'm a textbook case for the baby of the family. I found school completely boring and went out of my way not to go. I hated to read because I found it difficult, so I got put in a reading class with the kids who ate paste. Putting a book in front of me was the equivalent of a torture device. I couldn't even hope to compete with my straight-A, cheerleader older sister, or my near-perfect, athletic older brother. So I made a name for myself with my antics. I spent more time playing hooky to go fishing or crawling out of class when the teacher wasn't looking than sitting in my assigned seat. I was the kid who was always in trouble. So much so that even now, decades later, when someone raises their voice I run to the corner and stand there.

The other day at a flag football game, my wife called out, "Come on, Leman." Even though she said it in a nice tone, I flinched. I still felt nervous because every time someone said that when I was young, they were yelling at me. Like Pavlov's dogs, I got used to it.

School, for many lastborns, is merely a place to go because they have to be there. They can't hope to compete with their older siblings, so why try? That's why critical schooling elements for lastborns are fun, physical movement, and a lot of interaction with others. Without those, a baby will be quickly bored and decide school isn't worth his time and attention.

Take it from me. When my high school invited me back years later to put my name on their wall of fame, my mom accompanied me.

"Mom, we sure fooled a lot of people, didn't we?" I said.

She laughed and patted me on the arm. "We sure did."

"I got into so much trouble," I added, and started detailing some of the things I did while I was in school. Some she knew about, and others she didn't.

But nothing surprised my mom, nor was she fazed. "Honey, I'm so proud of you," she said. "I always knew you'd turn out."

What Can You Do for Your Lastborn?

- Make fun and physical movement an essential part of learning.
- Make social interaction and working in groups part of his schooling.
- Help him stay on task by spot-checking his projects and schedules when his attention wanders.
- Never do for him what he should do for himself.

That, parent, is what a lastborn needs most—your belief that he can become someone, in spite of who he may be right now.

He also needs to learn responsibility and accountability for his actions. Don't rescue him from homework he should do himself or take the blame for his failures when he drops the ball.

Yes, your lastborn will always major in fun and relationships, but he also needs to balance those desires with some hard academic work that he won't always feel like doing. It's a wonderful life lesson, since none of us gets to do what we want every minute of the day.

Now you be the psychologist for your home. Examine your kids closely and consider these questions:

- Is your child a serious, focus-on-studying individual? Is she highly competitive? Is he always asking questions? Does she have a penchant for science or math? Does he always need to know details about every event? Is she most comfortable knowing her road map—what middle school, high school, and college she'll be attending—early in life?

- Is your child peer oriented? Does he go with the flow and not get rattled? Is she the one least likely to be noticed if she's MIA?
- Is your child focused on fun and activities? Does he love interacting with others? Is she always up to something? Is it difficult for him to sit still in his seat because he likes being on the go? Does she not take no for an answer and keep pestering you until you give in?

Do you see why choosing specific schooling options for each individual child in your family will gain the best education perfectly suited to them?

Finding Just the Right Fit

In the story of Cinderella, three sisters try on a glass slipper. It's a perfect fit for only one of them. Looking for the right education options for each child is similar to that search for the owner of the glass slipper. Schools aren't a one-size-fits-all. You have to find the right fit for your child based on her unique learning styles, talents, personality, strengths, weaknesses, and present and future goals. Only you, parent, know your child that well to put together all those pieces.

Since kids tip their hand in these areas early in life, here are some questions you should ask yourself for starters:

- What is your child's activity level? Is he always on the go? Or can he tune in to playing with Legos or coloring and enjoy it?

97

- What is the length of your child's attention span? Can she focus on a single activity for hours? Or does she tend to jump from activity to activity?
- Does your child finish what he starts? Or does he tend to start multiple projects and not finish them?
- Is your child goal oriented, pushing through to the end even when something is difficult? Or does he tend to give up when a hurdle is placed in his path? Does he shut down when he has to compete with other scholars, especially if someone is not by his side to continually encourage him?
- Does your child constantly ask questions about how something works? Or does he tend to simply accept that something works?

The answers to these questions will give you a better idea of the schooling options you should pursue for your child.

Active children with shorter attention spans often have difficulty in book-learning classrooms. They need physical activity to wear off their excess energy before they can concentrate (though many schools have cut their PE programs). Those who already love books may be happy studying a subject for hours and even want to research additional materials on the subject.

If your child doesn't tend to finish what she starts or jumps from project to project, she'll likely have difficulty in settings where she is not monitored along the way. Then she won't reach her goals.

Children who falter when programs get difficult don't tend to do as well in high academic situations unless they have an encourager by their side. Those who are self-motivated and goal oriented often thrive in programs where they have ownership over how swiftly they can work and how much material they can cover.

Children who are curious about how things work often end up in math, science, or technology fields. They also can excel in vocational schools.

Following are a few examples of schooling matches that are good fits for your child's needs. There are numerous combinations, all based on a child's unique strengths and weaknesses and your family situation and beliefs.

A child in need of structure

You admit it. You've been a very permissive parent, and there isn't a lot of structure in your home. Your child has pretty much been able to do what he wants, and now he's clearly in need of structure.

Would it make sense to put him in a laissez-faire school that doesn't have a lot of guidelines and discipline? Where children work mainly on their own? Where they decide on their program plan and work at their own pace? Or would he be better suited to an environment that provides an overall plan and regular check-in points where he needs to stay on task?

A child who needs an even playing field

If it's important to you that your child is on an even playing field with other children in school, you might want to consider a school that has specific expectations and rules students have to adhere to, as well as a dress code.

Some public schools now have a dress code. It's not the traditional Catholic school plaid but more the Kohl's or Old Navy uniform pants and shirt. At the Leman Academy of Excellence, we don't have a set uniform that kids buy, because they come from a wide range of financial backgrounds. However, we do have basic color combinations that we expect the children to wear. Why make that a requirement? Because we don't want to create tension between kids whose parents have money and those whose parents don't, simply based on appearances. We want all kids to be on equal footing. If that's important to you too, consider a school with a dress code or uniforms. No, it might not make your fashion-conscious middle schooler happy, but it will likely win dividends by helping her focus on other things, such as getting to know students who are from different backgrounds.

A child who's not a stellar student

If you have a child who is currently a mediocre student in high school but says he wants to be a neurosurgeon, it's time to take a good look at his goals to see if what he says lines up with what he's done in the past and what he wants to do now. There's often a very big divide between the "ideal self" (what we want to be) and our "real self" (what we really are). If your child is an underachiever because he hasn't been properly motivated, that's one thing. If he is working hard but making average or below-average progress—especially in science and math, which he'd need for neurosurgery—it's doubtful he'll end up going that direction.

No, you don't want to crush any child's dream, but you don't want to reserve a place for him on the *Titanic* either.

Looking up what it takes to be a neurosurgeon—further classes and schooling—can bring reality to the situation and may prompt your child to take a realistic look at his skill set. If he has strong skills in a particular vocational direction, a vocational school may fit him better than the academically oriented private school he currently attends.

You don't want to crush any child's dream, but you don't want to reserve a place for him on the *Titanic* either.

A child who's orderly

If someone asked you to describe your child, and you said, "Orderly, very particular, likes things a certain way, wants to know the parameters of every project, works well within guidelines," then your child craves structure. He's not comfortable without it.

He may be a great fit for a high school military academy, but you should never put that child into a school system where the mantra is "discover your educational path" and "learn at your own pace." He'll be paralyzed by the lack of rules and guidelines.

A jack-of-all-trades

If your child is good at many things and a high achiever, she needs a school that allows her to explore different areas of interest besides the regular math, science, history, and English curriculum. She doesn't need a "just the basics" school. She needs one with art, music, language, and multiple other class options to choose from in order to discover specific passions.

If there is an area she'd like to explore that isn't on the school curriculum, why not add one activity per semester, whether it's a self-defense class, an acting class, or anything else that grabs her interest?

A child who's socially motivated

If your child is socially motivated, with academics being a backdrop, whatever schooling option you choose has to include lots of interaction with peers. Without that, your child won't stay interested in studying any topic for long.

Schools where he can work as part of a group to accomplish a goal will be very important. He's less likely to want to do a book report by himself than to contribute to a group book report. Also, lecture environments will be deadly. He needs to be able to bounce ideas around with his peers.

A child who needs hands-on learning

If your child will use any excuse not to pick up a book but loves to be in the science lab doing experiments, he needs a school that emphasizes active, hands-on learning—in other words, learning by doing. I would have done much better in a classroom that emphasized kinesthetic learning than a traditional classroom.

If your kid hates to read books—they feel too much like "work" to many kids—find internet articles in his subject of interest and drop intriguing facts about them. I guarantee his curiosity will tickle his fingers to google the topic and read that article. Not everybody is a reader, though it greatly helps in education.

102

One successful industrial engineer I know says he read precisely one book in his entire educational career while growing up. He scraped by in traditional school with Cs and Ds but found his calling in a shop class in eighth grade. That's where he discovered how much he loved to work with metal in crafting pieces that could work together as part of a larger whole. Now his company is known internationally for their precision, detail, and problem-solving ability.

Additional Considerations

Here are a few other things to consider when finding the right school for your child.

Exceptional needs

If your child could benefit from help with reading comprehension or her speech, needs wheelchair accessibility, or requires special transportation, you'll want to research school options that say they have such programs as well as how those programs are run. Are they add-ons to meet state regulations, or are they true programs, where your student's unique needs will be handled with individual attention and compassion?

Transportation and before- or after-school programs

If you're a working parent, transportation to school and back will be extremely important. Does the school have carpools? Buses? What are transportation costs, if any? Or is the parent responsible for getting their child to and from school?

In the state of New York, taxes are high. But if a child goes to a private school, he can be picked up by a public bus and taken to that school. Does the school you're looking into have any before- or after-school program where children are monitored if they need to be dropped off early or stay late?

Fit with family values

What values and beliefs are important to your family?

Is it important to you that the school's curriculum follows your faith beliefs? Or are you comfortable with different views being presented—for example, origins of the earth, gender issues—so that your child wades through all the options out there and can decide for himself what he believes?

Is the school family friendly? Do you want the option of taking your child on an extended trip as an add-on to his education? If so, does the school allow such leaves of absence? Are there exams after holidays or weekends? Leman Academy's policy is to make sure there are no exams following weekends, holidays, and vacations. Those times, we believe, are for families, and our school is big on partnering with families. Our philosophy is that parents are the best teachers. Yes, we will do a great job of educating your child. But we need your help, support, and understanding, and we want to work together with you to accomplish the goals of preparing your child not only in academics but also for mastering real life.

Outside activities

What's the best mix of "regular school" and "outside school" activities? A lot of that depends on the schooling menu options you choose and how important spending time together as a family is to you. Some families are comfortable with running from place to place, with fast-food options for dinner.

Is that necessarily the best thing? You tell me. How do you feel after you run around crazily for even one day? How do you think your child feels? That's why I always suggest that parents don't overschedule their kids and, if their kids are older, don't allow them to overschedule themselves. There are only so many hours in a day, and everyone needs time to breathe.

Your scholar has two primary jobs while she's in school and living in your home—to be a student and to be an active participant in your family. All other activities should be considered extras and carefully reviewed. Are they simply filling time, or are they exploring real interests and developing skills that will help set up your child to live well in the future? If your child is constantly sidelined or bench sitting in an extracurricular activity, why not try something else where she can be an active participant?

> **Your scholar has two primary jobs while she's in school and living in your home—to be a student and to be an active participant in your family.**

The Triangle Effect

Education is never a one-person show. It's all about a team—parents, child, and teacher. Yes, the administrator counts too, but you and your child don't interact with that person every day. That means no matter who your child's teacher is, you have some responsibilities as a member of the team. You'll have a much better partnership if you do the following:

Education a la Carte

- Communicate to the teacher that you want to support him in the classroom in any way you possibly can. Ask about any particular needs you might be able to help with—volunteering for field trips or class parties, or assisting reluctant readers or children who are "differently abled." Don't just focus on your own child's needs. Become your teacher's helper in ways you're able to.

- Fill your teacher in on things she needs to know about your child to help him learn most effectively—personality, learning style, and motivations you've noticed. Such knowledge will greatly help a teacher who is just getting introduced to your child.

  For example, "My son tends to respond better when he's prompted. As a mom, I've discovered that the higher you push the bar, the more he'll work hard. If not, he'll slack off." That will be particularly important information for a more laid-back teacher to know, because otherwise your student might underperform in her class.

  That method, though, doesn't work for all kids. Some will wilt right before your eyes if you install a high-jump bar in front of them. Others will get a gleam in their eyes, ready for the challenge. Knowing how your child responds to educational challenges is critical for both you and the teacher.

- Have your teacher's back. Form a bond that says to him, "I believe you can bring out the best in my kid. I know there are some things you as a third party can do that I can't, because I'm also his parent. I'm all for growing my child, and I'll support you. If there is an

106

issue I'm unsure about, I'll come to you first. If there is a misunderstanding, I want to work it through with you. I won't jump to conclusions, even if my child is upset about something that happened in class."

Those three basics will get you, the teacher, and your child on the same page so you can start the school year off positively.

Teachers today don't get a lot of respect across the board. So trust me when I say that your child's teacher needs a friend, and you can be that friend. Just don't be a meddling friend or one who expects favors (it's not okay for your child to fail a test or miss completing an assignment just because you and the teacher are on good terms). It doesn't need to be you and your child against the teacher. It should be all of you working together to get the best possible education for your child.

Whose Education Is It?

You can do all you can to ensure the right schooling options for your child and have a great teacher to match. But don't forget whose education it is—your child's. He has to do his part too. He has to be willing to learn and to engage in the process.

Every child wants to be somebody. But the question is, what kind of somebody do they want to be? And how hard are they willing to work to get there?

When I travel, I run into all kinds of families. Recently I met a family in which all four siblings—three brothers and one sister—are physicians. Imagine! How does that happen?

Well, guess what their dad is. Yes, a physician. Guess what their grandpa was. Yes, a physician.

It all has to do with the values of a family that are poured into the children from the get-go. When family values are strong—in that family, the emphasis is on helping others through medical practice and research—sometimes the children will fall in line and all become high achievers.

But here's what's fascinating. Even with all four children in the medical field, they don't go head-to-head in the same branch. You still see their individuality and uniqueness. One is a pediatrician, one is a cardiologist, one is in high-level medical research and earning a second doctorate, and one is in geriatric medicine. I can just imagine the discussions those siblings have over the Thanksgiving turkey and the holiday ham. I'm sure they're way past my ability to even process.

> "School is your work. It's your chance to shine. It's your education. I'll do my best to encourage and help you along the way, but what you decide to do with the opportunities is up to you."

All of us have responsibilities in life. Your child's largest responsibility right now is attending school. If he doesn't want to be there, a frank discussion is in order.

"I know you hate school right now. You think it's worthless. But a huge majority of those who get ahead in life have an education. Every day I get up at 6:00 a.m., and I'm at my job by 8:00. I work until 6:00 p.m. That's the nature of my job. You have a job too, and that's school. You're there seven hours a day, so you might as well make the best of your time. Someday you're going to graduate from high school. When you get your diploma, a name will be on it. It will be yours, not mine. School is your work. It's your chance to shine. It's your education. I'll do my best to encourage and help you along the way, but what you decide to do with the opportunities is up to you."

Let me say it bluntly. For any education option to work, your child has to be willing to make it work. You can select the right dishes from the menu, but you can't make your kids eat them.

What makes all the difference in the world is your relationship with your child. If it's based on love, trust, and mutual respect, you can work together to assemble an a la carte menu that your child won't be able to resist.

Learning will be easy but challenging . . . and most of all, fun.

5

Your Parental Role in Schooling

*How your background, expectations, and beliefs
influence your definition of your child's success.*

You, parent, hold a wonderful ace card. That card is you. What you think and believe and the way you live have everything to do with your child's educational success. Your child is watching you more than anyone else in the world, and that glimpse of you forms a great deal of his worldview. That's why, in order to choose the best schooling options for your child, it's important to take a good look at your own background, expectations, and beliefs. What is your view of education? Your parenting style? Your personality? And how do those influence your child and his perspective on schooling?

Your View of Education

Years ago I did a research study on perceived parental attitudes toward higher education. The net result was clear: a child's success in college has everything to do with a parent's attitude toward higher education. Parents who value education will likely be natural encouragers of their children in regard to getting an excellent education and taking it seriously. After all, they've had experiences with education (or the lack of it) and have come to realize its benefits.

But here's what's interesting. Having parents who were highly educated didn't make the difference. It was the parents' *attitude* toward schooling in general that was the predictor of success.

Take Ben Carson, a poor kid from a tough neighborhood who became a lauded surgeon. When he was 11, he was failing school. His older brother, Curtis, wasn't doing much better. Sonya, his single mother, only had a third-grade education but wanted a different life for her sons. On top of their regular schoolwork, she required them to read two books per week and write reports on them, which they would turn in to her. What the boys didn't know until years later was that their own mother didn't know how to read.

> A child's success in college has everything to do with a parent's attitude toward higher education.

Within a year, Ben had moved from the very bottom of his class to the top. Later he would receive a scholarship to Yale University, be accepted as a resident at Johns Hopkins Hospital, and then become a neurosurgeon so skilled that he was able to separate conjoined baby twins, saving both of their lives.

That young mom could have given up on her boys and let them continue to be hooked on television nonstop. Instead, she valued education because she knew it could change their lives . . . and it did.

Valuing education isn't an attitude you put on like a piece of clothing your child's junior year of high school, when you both start thinking about college. It's a mind-set you've adopted—a desire for your children to have a better life than you've had. Education is one of the best ways to help close that gap. Articulating to your children that school is important and that teachers deserve respect and attention is a huge start in the right direction.

Your Parenting Style

Have you ever said, "I will never say what my dad [mom] said to me," but then you say it not only multiple times but with the same inflection and volume? That's because old patterns really do stick.

The way you respond to your kids and their educational challenges often resembles how your parents responded to you. Every parent tends toward one of three styles, which greatly influences how your child does in school.

Authoritarian

Do you do the following?

- Lay down the law to your child. "You better study . . . or else."
- Check up on him to make sure he's following the rules.

- Dictate her study time—what she should do and when.
- Make your child's decisions for him. "Of course you're going to be on the quiz team this semester. You always are."
- Redo projects for your child because they're not good enough.
- Keep an eye on your child's schedule, telling her when projects are due.

If this is the way you tend to respond, then your parenting style is that of an authoritarian, and you'll tend to micromanage your kids. You likely learned that style from your father, since many authoritarians are males—especially those who grew up with strict backgrounds—and you fell easily into it when you had your own children.

Parents need to focus on developing discerning thinkers who can stand firm on their own and creatively problem solve.

The authoritarian parenting style seems to work—at least in the short term. However, the long-term results are not ones that lead to educational or life success. Authoritarian parenting breeds

- outward compliance but inward rebellion (which tends to come out later, when the child gains more independence from you)
- obnoxious, rude, argumentative behavior since the child must work hard to gain some space for herself
- the inability to think independently

- the inability to be spontaneous, since all of life has been planned out for him
- little creativity in problem solving—everything is seen in black and white
- the stress of every small thing becoming a major thing (Bs are seen as Ds)

Children who are parented by one or more authoritarians tend to rely on others to make decisions for them. Without authority directly over them, life can feel frightening and out of control. In today's global world, parents need to focus on developing discerning thinkers who can stand firm on their own and creatively problem solve.

Permissive

Do you do the following?

- Rescue your child from consequences.
- Go out of your way to defend and back him, even if he's done wrong.
- Complete homework for her when she feels overwhelmed.
- Problem solve every situation so he doesn't have to be inconvenienced.
- Apologize for her temper.
- Always make life "easy" for him.
- Overindulge her with too many gifts and "me-centered" activities.

If this is the way you tend to respond, then your parenting style is that of a permissive parent, and you'll major in making excuses for your kids. You have difficulty holding your child accountable to complete her work. In fact, you feel bad when she struggles with anything, so you tend to do her homework for her if you catch even a whiff of complaint that "It's too hard." And that project for the science fair? It isn't her work; it's yours.

You likely learned the permissive parenting style from one of your parents (probably your mother), and it also seems to work—at least in the short term. You feel good doing all you can to help your child, and your child's life seems to be easier than the one you had, because you're snowplowing all the roads for her. However, permissive parenting breeds

- guilt in the child for getting away with so much
- an overemphasis on the value of stuff
- self-centeredness because he always gets his way
- the inability to develop relationships due to lack of consideration and caring for others
- the inability to realize the consequences of actions
- little restraint when going after things your child wants (if another person gets hurt, so what?)

Children who are parented by one or more permissive parents may be cushioned for a while, but they are smacked in the face by real life when they are away from Mommy and Daddy's protective nest. Then they struggle with great difficulty in their jobs, especially with keeping them, as they don't play well on teams. They tend to have short fuses when

115

> **Those who succeed in life do so because they learn how to work hard, accept failure as a part of life and learn from it, and then push on to excellence.**

life doesn't go well for them. And they won't rise to the top academically because they expect to be rescued. So studying last minute and ineffectually preparing is the name of the game.

Permissive parents don't do their kids any favors in the short term or in the long term. Those who succeed in life do so because they learn how to work hard, accept failure as a part of life and learn from it, and then push on to excellence.

Authoritative

Do you do the following?

- Present things as they are.
- Ask your child for the facts before jumping to any conclusions.
- Let reality be the teacher instead of lecturing your child.
- Allow him to experience consequences.
- Work with her to develop good study habits.
- Expect your child to do his own work when it's due.
- Provide age-appropriate choices and allow your child to make her own decisions.

If this is the way you tend to respond, then you're an authoritative parent. You have a healthy balance of being your child's parent and allowing your child to be an individual. After establishing family guidelines for behavior, you trust your child to do what's right. You don't need to follow up to hold him accountable. He knows what you expect, and most of the time he meets and even exceeds those expectations (though children are still humans and sometimes drop the ball).

Authoritative parenting breeds

- good decision-making skills
- respect, confidence, and self-worth
- the ability to stick by decisions
- a hard-work ethic
- the ability to stand straight even in strong winds
- the drive to study hard and to succeed

The best way you can help your child succeed is through authoritative parenting—making expectations clear, trusting your child to meet them, and respecting your child's individuality. For example, some children need a break after school before they start studying. They might work best on homework from 8:00 to 10:00 p.m. Others need to tackle it right away. So why dictate when your child will do homework if she is getting it done, and done well? If you articulate that school is important and you have an authoritative parenting style, your child will naturally adopt that same worldview.

Your Personality

As you look at schooling options for your child, it's important to know the pluses and minuses of your own personality. Are you a controller? A pleaser? A charmer? A victim? All of these ways of thinking and reacting will impact the way you respond to your child's education.

The controller

You crave order and don't do well in chaos. You like to be in charge. Because you have high expectations of yourself, you expect the same of others. You like to work alone so that others don't mess up what you do. You're not a person who rolls with the punches because you don't like surprises. You can also tend to have a temper when things don't go your way.

> Out of love for your child, you need to consider all education options carefully, with *your child's* best in mind.

Controllers always have a plan in mind—a specific schooling option they want their kids to kowtow to. Problem is, every person is an individual. Your child may be different from you in every way. What pushed you to succeed—an intense, controlled environment—might crush your fun-loving, social daughter. Out of love for your child, you need to consider all education options carefully, with *your child's* best in mind.

What a controller wants most is respect.

What about your child? Is he a controller? If so, that will affect the type of schooling you choose. A laissez-faire environment would drive him crazy.

The pleaser

Pleasers most often are women. Do you go out of your way to make other people happy? Do you sometimes take the blame for things that aren't your fault? Sometimes you let others run over you because you rarely stand up for yourself. You give others a lot of leeway, but they take advantage of you.

My mother was a pleaser—kindhearted and gullible. So many times from ages 10 to 12, I went out the door and she truly believed with all of her heart that I was going to school. I might even have taken a book with me, just to make it look good, but I didn't go to school. I went fishing. The night before, I'd hidden my fishing rod across the street in the tall grass.

Even though my mom was a nurse and technically knew better, all I had to do was look a little uncomfortable in the morning and feign a stomachache, and she'd say, "What's wrong, honey? Is it high or low?"

I never did know why she'd ask, "Is it high or low?" but she was a nurse, so there had to be a reason. I couldn't care less as long as I didn't have to go to school.

Truth is, I was a lying duck. I knew how to easily bail out of school in my own way by using my manipulative personality. Even more, because my mom was also a baby of the family, she always had a soft heart for my plight as a baby—and fell for that manipulation.

If you're a pleaser, you'll find yourself doing your child's homework, writing excuse notes for your child that aren't really true, and snowplowing his roads in life in other ways. Like my sweet mama, you'll allow yourself to be manipulated.

But if you don't stand up for yourself and learn to say no to your child's manipulation, you're teaching your child that every adult can be manipulated in such a way. When he tries it with his math teacher after not turning in his homework for the second day in a row, how do you think that will work? Enough said.

What a pleaser wants most is to be appreciated. But your child will never appreciate you if he can manipulate you.

What about your child? Is she a pleaser? If so, that will affect the type of schooling you choose. A highly structured environment might crush her forward path academically.

The charmer

Charmers are those who crave being the center of attention. I wish I had time and space to tell you how I talked my way into Disneyland . . . for free. And not for one ticket but for nine. When I think of things I've done in life, that's got to be close to the top. Do you desire the limelight? Do you like to make people laugh? You're probably an extrovert, like me. You don't like to be treated as insignificant or ignored. If you don't get your way, you might pout or even get angry. When life doesn't go your way, you are a little paralyzed, because you're used to getting what you want.

What the charmer wants most is affection.

What about your child? Is she a charmer? If so, that will affect the type of schooling you choose. Your child will need a healthy balance of guidelines and structure, as well as a highly social environment, in order to succeed.

The victim

Victims are those who feel like life is unjust. Do you feel like you got a raw deal? Do you tend to resent where you are in life? Do you wonder why you didn't get the same educational advantages as others? You also might think that you're always the one who will be blamed if something goes wrong. The mantra of your life is, "I guess I'm just unlucky."

You feel most comfortable when people are sympathetic toward you. One of your favorite statements from adult friends is, "Oh, I don't know how you do it all." However, your lack of self-confidence and worth won't help your child gain self-worth or give him the extra drive to push ahead in school. Nor will it help you find ways to assist your child educationally with the right match for his talents. If you don't think *you* can succeed, how will he think *he* can succeed? The old saying is true: the apple doesn't fall far from the tree.

What a victim wants most is pity.

What about your child? Does he have a victim mentality, thinking that everyone else has gotten a better deal in life? If so, that will affect the type of schooling you choose. Your child won't have internal motivation and a desire to succeed because he already thinks he'll be a failure. So he'll need an encouraging environment but one that holds him accountable for moving ahead step-by-step.

Academic Basics You Should Expect of Your Children

- Work independently.
- Do homework by themselves (or with minimal supervision).
- Contribute equally to group projects.
- Ask for help when they truly don't understand a subject.
- Study the material they will be tested over to the best of their ability.

Why You Parent the Way You Do, and How That Influences Your View of Education

Just as birth order has everything to do with who your child is and how he'll respond to schooling options, it also has everything to do with why you parent the way you do and your educational expectations for your child.

If you're a firstborn

Since you're a perfectionist, you take education very seriously, so your child better do the same. Seeing As on your child's report card is extremely important to you and, frankly, is nonnegotiable. Academic progress is much more valuable to you than social interaction.

You also expect your child to be well organized, a list maker, a natural leader, and conscientious about getting his homework done. To you, there's a right way to do things, and anything else is wrong. That's why it drives you crazy when your kids don't study with the same intensity you would. You tend to undo what your child does on a project so you can do it "better."

If you're an onlyborn

Since you're a high achiever, self-motivated, and a great reader, you expect the same of your child. You can't imagine her not doing every project thoroughly. Because you've always worked independently, you don't think of checking in on your child's academic progress to keep her motivated. You demand excellence in all areas and expect her to be top dog in her area of expertise. Failure is not an option.

You also don't understand why siblings would fight and compete with each other, or why they would need to go to different schools. *Just pick the best school,* you think, *and send all the kids there. It's logical. Simple. And they get a top-notch education.*

If you're a middleborn

When your child gets a low grade on her report card or doesn't do well in a performance, you smooth the event over with your controlling spouse or the grandparent who pays private-school tuition. You go out of your way to avoid conflicts, always acting as diplomatic mediator between your child and the teacher or administration.

Your child attending a school where she can interact easily with peers and develop a solid network of friends is very important to you—likely more so than the academic environment.

If you're a lastborn

Making sure your child is having fun and is happy is your top priority. That's why you go out of your way to "help" him with his homework. Having time to play and explore is valuable to you, so you tend to let your baby of the family get away with anything.

The social environment of a school is very important to you. So are additional activities in which your child can get involved for a broader school experience.

Identifying with your birth order

As much as you try to make your relationship with your children "equal and the same," there will always be one who is your favorite and one you always want to knock off their perch because the two of you clash so much. Why is that? Because parents tend to overidentify with the child of the same birth order.

> As much as you try to make your relationship with your children "equal and the same," there will always be one who is your favorite and one you always want to knock off their perch because the two of you clash so much.

For example, let's say you are homeschooling. If you're a firstborn, you'll put a lot of pressure and expectations on your firstborn because that's how you were treated. If you're a middleborn, you'll make life easiest on your middleborn by smoothing his educational pathway. If you're a baby of the family, you'll find ways to excuse your lastborn's antics and lack of push to do his homework.

See how it works? The more you understand about birth order, the more you'll be able to provide balanced parenting *and* choose the right schooling options.

The Single Greatest Factor in Success . . . or Failure

I'll be blunt. What can swing the balance most in academic and life excellence or failure is parental criticism. Are you a flaw picker? Always denigrating what your child does as not good enough or pushing him to be better? If he gets a 96 on a test, do you say, "You should have gotten a 100"?

If your kids constantly have to jump over the high bar in order to make you proud, the problem isn't with them. It's with you. Are you, at your core, insecure? Are you trying to fulfill your own desires through projecting them onto your child? If so, that's a lot of stress to put on both of you. Flaw picking to your child is like an umpire constantly yelling to a batter, "Three strikes and you're out!"

If you constantly criticize, you'll gain a child who

- often procrastinates, because he's afraid of being evaluated
- thinks negatively of herself and criticizes herself endlessly for even a small mistake
- can't forget failures
- feels like he is always letting you down
- can never enjoy life, because she always thinks she could be doing better
- believes he can never measure up
- doesn't trust any good thing people say about her
- has little self-confidence to forge ahead
- can never see himself as successful, because he's always waiting to be exposed as the loser his parents portray him to be

There is a difference between having standards of excellence and asking your child to jump too high or too low, based on her individual gifts. If your child comes to you and asks for help, then help. But if you're still there 45 minutes later, and you and your child are both in tears or angry, the situation clearly isn't working. As the parent, you need to make a judgment call. Are you being sucked in and manipulated by your child? If so, it's time to do things differently.

125

How Do Your Beliefs Play into the Mix?

If you are a person of a specific faith or religious background and it is critically important to you that your child's education closely follows your beliefs, your schooling options are more limited. However, let me caution you on one thing. A school may say it follows a certain faith, but does it really? Is that Christian school as "Christian" as it claims? Sadly, there are popular Christian schools whose leaders are anything but Christian. Behind all the glossy brochures, they're masters of deceit. On the other hand, there are some great Christian schools out there. Recently I visited a large one in Fort Lauderdale, Florida, and walked away greatly impressed by the high academics and the way they competed in major sports with citywide teams. It's a school of passion and excellence.

> There is a difference between having standards of excellence and asking your child to jump too high or too low, based on her individual gifts.

So before you jump on board—even if the brochure or website says it's a Hebrew school, Muslim school, parochial school, or denominational school—check it out carefully yourself. Do you agree with the school's philosophy on paper? Visit the school in person before you even get your child involved in the possibility. When you walk the hallways and talk with the teachers, can you see your child being comfortable in that environment? (It's a red flag if they don't allow you to visit the school and interact with the faculty and staff.)

No school is perfect. But choosing a school to replace what you should be teaching at home is a big mistake.

You should always rear your kids in such a way that they understand your family's faith and values, which are not only taught in verbal form but also caught through your role modeling.

Every kid should learn to be cognizant of others' thoughts, feelings, and ideas. They should be steered clear of the false assumption that they are the center of the universe— the way most people raise their kids. If you do these things, you set up your child to develop a real, lasting faith

> No school is perfect. But choosing a school to replace what you should be teaching at home is a big mistake.

that includes living out the virtues you hold dear. After all, if your child thinks he's the center of the universe, where's the place for Almighty God?

What Are Your Expectations for Your Kids?

Let's face it. All of us have expectations for our kids that are both realistic and unrealistic regarding their education. Those expectations are based on our backgrounds and our experiences as parents, both positive and negative. They have a lot to do with our own parents' view of education and their treatment of our failures and successes.

If you went to college and graduate school, you likely want your child to follow the same path. You know what you had to do to succeed academically, so you have the road map down. However, stop for a second and remember that your child is an individual. She needs to discover some things for herself, such as how to balance her time, the value of hard work, and what skills are uniquely hers. You telling her what to do and how to do it won't necessarily speed things up. It will actually do the opposite—slow her progress because she's not learning for herself.

You may be driven by the pressure to succeed and be driving your child in the same direction. But where does your definition of success come from? And why are you "keeping up with the Joneses" anyway? Just who are they, and why are they shaping your life and your child's? Why not allow for individuality in your search for academic excellence?

Your expectations for your child don't need to be like anybody else's. So ask yourself these questions:

- Are my expectations for my child reasonable? Would I have liked the same ones when I was growing up?
- Are my rules flexible or inflexible? (Too much change, and your kids won't know what to expect. Too little change, and you're over the top with perfectionism.)
- Are my schooling goals based on my real child or the ideal child I'm projecting?

Perfectionism won't do you or your child any favors. Your expectations need to fit who your child really is. They also need to be framed in terms of a healthy, loving relationship between the two of you.

When your child struggles with school, yes, you should provide assistance. But make sure it's respectful of your child and gives him credit for doing his part. Saying things like, "I'm sure you can handle this work. I believe in you. I trust your judgment and know you'll take care of this situation to the best of your ability," solidifies that respect.

But in the midst of helping your child, never rescue him from consequences. Just as you don't shovel out his garbage-aroma room because he hasn't gotten around to it, you shouldn't accept the consequences for shoddy academic work. If you're a perfectionist, his room will never be clean enough for you anyway. And everything he does at school— even if he's on the honor roll—won't be enough either. You'll always be pushing him higher and further.

Nobody likes to be micromanaged. Would you like someone picking out your clothes? Then why are you directing what your child should wear? Unless, of course, she's at a school that has specific rules for clothing. Then again, if your child rebels and chooses not to follow the guidelines one day, why is it your problem? Just let the school handle it. If your child gets sent home to change, it's doubtful she'll do that again.

> **Nobody likes to be micromanaged.**

Let's say your daughter just bombed a trigonometry test. Math has always been her strong point, but this time you happen across the F on the test paper in her backpack. How do you handle that disappointment?

First of all, why were you snooping in her backpack? If you have a good relationship with your daughter, then you trust her . . . and wait for her to tell you in her own timing. Snooping in her backpack shows that you don't have respect for her, nor do you trust her. So why would she want to tell you?

Second, if your daughter didn't tell you about the F, could it be because she didn't have the nerve? Because she feared your reaction—that you'd freak out over the grade? Or she was afraid to disappoint you? Perhaps she's so disappointed in herself that she doesn't need anybody else harping on her failure.

Third, whose F is it? Even though you know she spent the evening before the test staying up too late, texting friends, and watching YouTube videos, and probably didn't effectively study, is that your problem? No, it's hers. If you don't rescue her or harp on her, she'll have to take responsibility for those actions herself.

It's better to be honest and say, "Honey, I need to ask you to forgive me. I happened to see your test grade. I'm sorry. Your backpack isn't my property, and I shouldn't have snooped. Please forgive me." Then look her in the eye. "I know you. You're probably beating yourself up a lot over that grade. But I also trust you to do what's right. It's one test, and it's not the end of the world. Maybe we'll both learn something." And you turn your back and walk away.

You can imagine the shock on your daughter's face. She expected to get hammered. Instead, you've shown her the mercy that you wished your parents had extended to you. Most of all, you've improved your relationship. You've admitted that you sometimes fail too, and put you and your child on the same playing field.

How to Win Your Child's Heart

You may wonder, especially in the turbulent adolescent and teen years, what has happened to the kid who used to love curling up in your lap and spending time with you. Now he has peach fuzz on his face. And the closest he wants you to get is 15 steps behind him, if you even have to be on the same street at all. As your child changes and his individuality grows, it will be critical that you allow him to mature, and that can include a change in schooling options as well.

No matter what education options you choose or how your child progresses academically, don't forget to pay attention to his heart. How can you best do that?

Put things in proper perspective.

So a kid blows off a paper, bombs a test, or underperforms at a concert or game. Maybe she had a fight with her best friend. Or the girl he likes just declared she likes someone else. If this is a onetime event, don't major in it. If it's a continuing event, it's time to start asking some questions.

It's a lucky kid who knows their parent will keep things in perspective and thus can talk to them about anything. Parents don't get to that treasured spot by calling out a kid for a mistake, ripping on a teacher for being incapable, or whining about how unfair a test is. They get there by active listening and not making molehills into mountains.

Yes, you should have your kid's back. You should listen to his perspective and opinion. You should protect her when she needs protection. You need to remain solidly in your child's court. But you should also always allow the balls of responsibility to fall on the proper side of the court.

Allow your child to be an individual.

Just because you do something one way doesn't mean your child has to do it the same way. Your ideas don't have to be your child's ideas. He is accountable for his own behavior.

Think of yourself as your child's personal trainer. You can walk alongside her and coach her, but you can't do the physical work for her. If you want your child to have strong psychological muscles, she needs to do the heavy lifting. That goes double for a child's own dreams and goals.

Don't let your fears control your expectations.

If you struggled with academics or parental expectations, some of these concerns might sound familiar:

- "I hated school, and now my younger child has a big problem with reading. I struggled with it too, so how can I help her? I want to, but I don't feel capable since I failed at it myself."
- "I was always a good student, but my parents flipped out when I got a D once in geography, something I'm horrible at. My middle child seems to have no interest in academics. The only thing that's important to him is his friend network. How can I encourage him to pay attention to academics? He'll never get into a college the way he's going."
- "I never was good at math. Even the math my sixth grader is doing now is beyond me. How can I best help her? I'm considering homeschooling, but I don't feel confident I could handle the math."

Maybe you weren't good at school. Or you could pass every subject except one or two, where you failed miserably. But should that limit the schooling options open to you? You don't have to be good at everything. You just have to be smart about seeking out resources where you're weak.

Or maybe you were so good at school that your child can never measure up. No matter your background and experiences, you have to set aside your own prejudices and fears in order to pursue what's best for your child.

Don't project your unfulfilled dreams or wishes onto your child.

I'll be blunt. If everything you do in life revolves around your kid and his success, you need to get a life for yourself. The worst thing you can do to your kids is try to fulfill your own dreams through them.

My father, who only graduated from the eighth grade, told all three of his kids, "Remember, you have to go to the big school." To him, "the big school" meant college. My sister heard that expectation right. She never got a B in her life. Neither did my brother. They both excelled in academics. But apparently I wasn't listening well. I didn't go that way . . . at least not for a long time.

Yes, you might lack education. And you realize how many things can stack up against you because you don't have the golden Willy Wonka ticket of a post–high school degree. There's no parent alive who doesn't wish for a better life for their kid. But "a better life" doesn't mean the same life.

So many parents live vicariously through their kids. Melanie was told she had great musical talent in grade school, but she ended up quitting music lessons because she got tired of all the extra hard work. She always felt guilty about not developing those skills and wondered what her life would have been like

Education a la Carte

if she had. When her 8-year-old started taking piano, Melanie was over the top in her expectations, pushing her daughter to excel. When her daughter wanted to quit six months into the lessons, that didn't go over well with Mama. Her daughter continued to take lessons for three more years, growing more and more emotionally fragile from the intensity and stress until she fell apart in the middle of a solo recital.

> There's no parent alive who doesn't wish for a better life for their kid. But "a better life" doesn't mean the same life.

I remember once sitting at a Bobby Sox game. A mother who was a PhD candidate in psychology was being a pain in the keister to the entire crowd. Every time her kid got up to bat, there was a constant barrage of her yelling, "Lower your left shoulder. Get your elbow out. Choke up on the bat." It was such a constant harassment of the kid that everybody in the stands got annoyed. When the kid didn't make a hit and grounded out, popped out, or struck out, I could hear the mom's exasperated moan from 10 rows away.

All I could think was, *What is her PhD in? Stupidity?*

Truth is, if there is a problem, a child can usually figure it out on his own. If reality is allowed to do the talking, the consequences take care of themselves. Parents are often the ones who need common sense—at least, that's what many teachers and principals tell me, after personal appointments with parents who've gone ballistic and threatened to sue because their kids weren't being treated properly.

Most kids don't like attention drawn to them. They want to take care of things themselves, not have a bunch of adults do it for them.

134

Think the best, not the worst.

If you stay positive, even in negative situations, you retain a strong, healthy relationship with your child that will extend beyond the time he is in your home. When you have a good relationship, you can nicely call a spade a spade, but you don't use it to dig your kids' grave in the backyard, nor do you use it to dig up the bones of previous failures. When your child bombs that test, you might say in an even tone, "There must have been some curveballs on that test—some questions that you didn't have a clue were going to be on there—for you to get a 56."

One blown test doesn't mean your child will blow life. If you respond in such an understated way and don't harp on the failure, you stay close to your child. You also open the door to conversation if your daughter decides she wants it.

If you want to stay in the parental ball game, don't leave the field or throw a tantrum. In baseball, if a coach overdoes it, he gets thrown out of the game. A demonstrative fist in the air, the donnybrook starts, and that coach gets sent to the dugout. Once there, he can't tell the players what to do any longer.

That's why it's so important for you to stay on the field and to keep your head in the game. Sometimes you won't understand what your kid does. But instead of starting a donnybrook between you and your child and ousting yourself from the game, simply say, "Honey, I don't understand. I'm willing to try, but you're going to have to shed some light on this matter, because I'm clueless."

It's true. You don't know everything. The sooner you admit that, and open your ears and shut your mouth about the

135

event, the faster you'll find out what really happened. Your kids don't really care what you know or what you think until they know that you care.

Remember that trust and respect are both two-way streets. Take advantage of the times when your child wants to talk with you. If he desires to engage in conversation, you've likely done a good job of active listening throughout his life. Realize that he's talking because he trusts you so much that he wants to process with you. Him asking, "What do you think, Mom [Dad]?" is the ultimate compliment to you as a parent.

> If you want to stay in the parental ball game, don't leave the field or throw a tantrum.

Rearing children who love to learn is an art form. It doesn't happen instantly but is a by-product of the kind of parent who puts a high emphasis on learning, provides a home and school environment that is conducive to learning, and has a warm, balanced relationship with their child.

Remember that everyone in the family has a job.

It's important that each member of the family has a specific role and that the role is clearly stated. For example, "This family works together and plays together. I work at the corporation downtown. Dad has his own restaurant. School is your job. You go to high school and play soccer. Your brother attends middle school and takes drum lessons. Your little sister is in first grade and is taking a painting class. We all come home at night and have certain responsibilities. Sometimes that's fixing dinner, cleaning the family room,

The Seven Best Things Parents Can Do to Help Their Child Succeed

1. Stay close but not too close. Know what's going on, but don't be a snoop.
2. Engage with his interests. Solicit his knowledge and opinions.
3. Don't do things that she can do for herself.
4. Don't accept excuses. They only make your child weak.
5. Focus on listening rather than talking.
6. Be open to change.
7. Realize that your child's life is his, not yours. Support his dreams and goals.

or doing dishes. We all pull our weight at home and at school." As everyone contributes, their place in the family remains secure and unique. And as each child focuses on their particular talents, based on schooling options suited to them, they begin to see their broader role—that they truly can make the planet a better place by contributing their unique gifts.

Make life a teachable moment.

Take an active interest in what your child is learning. Your job isn't to know everything. Nor is it to pummel your child with questions to see what he knows. If you see your son's science project but don't understand it, say, "Hey, what an interesting project. I'm not sure what it's all about, but I'd love to know." With such words you open the door to conversation.

"Oh, it's about the weather, and at what temperature water freezes and then becomes liquid again," your son explains.

You don't need to have a PhD in science. In fact, science could have been your worst subject in school. All you have to say is, "Wow, I'm really impressed with your time and effort. It must feel good to do all that research and figure out how to create that project." Such active interest not only encourages your science-oriented child but also grows your relationship.

So why not look naturally for opportunities to turn news and information into teachable moments?

Let's say you're at a nearby farm, and your child asks, "Mommy, what are the horses doing in the pasture?"

You have a choice. You can hide your daughter's eyes from the boy and girl horses that are doing the mambo, or you can explain the basics of conception in age-appropriate terms. If your child wants to know more, she'll let you know. When her curiosity is satisfied, she'll stop asking questions.

When you take advantage of such natural learning, you're passing on both information and values. You're telling your child that sex is something you can discuss. It's not unnatural or dirty or something to be hidden. You're opening the door to your child asking you further questions about any subject she's curious about. Ditto with events you hear about on the news, such as racial prejudice, rape, and murder. With even young children today having internet access, she will hear about all kinds of things happening in the news, much earlier than you ever did. Isn't it best that she's able to process them with you at her side, through the lens of values you hold dear?

In doing this, you're satisfying your child's curiosity in a way that opens the door to a continued drive for knowledge. Also, you're providing the framework for her to discover new information and make good decisions based on clearly defined family values.

As your child matures, you can say, "Honey, you know my and Dad's opinion on that. You've heard it a lot over the years. But you know what's most important? That you make the right decision for you."

When you have a good relationship, your child translates your words as, "Wow. She cares how I feel and what I think, and she listens to me. She trusts me to make a good decision."

That puts you on the same page with your child not only in natural education at home and in her schooling options along the way, but in all of life.

6

Preschool and Kindergarten

How to know if your child is ready for these first steps.

One of the questions I'm asked most frequently about early childhood education is, "How much do we push, and how early?" If you are the parent of young children, this is likely a hot question on your mind. (If your children are older, you have my permission to skip this chapter. Or you can read it out of curiosity.)

Pushing education is never a good idea—ever. Let's be honest. When you're forced to do something, do you like it, or the person forcing you to do it? Then why would you push the first steps of schooling on your child?

Some parents are already trying to chart their child's career by the time he's in kindergarten. Their focus is firmly fixed on getting their child into the "best" and "right" schools to make him a success. But nothing in life is a guarantee, and you set up both yourself and your child for a big fall if there's any hitch in your plans.

It's a Wide, Wonderful World Out There

Instead of trying to pin a career on your child who has just recently begun walking, why not focus on introducing him to the most wonderful world of learning from babyhood on? The younger your child, the more of a sponge he is. But how exactly can you make such an introduction?

One way is very easy. You start by reading to your kids when they're young. You show a *Pat the Bunny* book to your 6-month-old. You let her hold it, even if she chews on the edges, drools on it, and ruffles the pages with her fingers. That's the point of exploratory, natural learning anyway. Later those tooth marks and crinkled, drool-stained spots will hold treasured memories for you when you're in your rocker and reverting to drooling yourself. Some baby books even have mirrors in them where a baby can see herself, identify who she is, and then point to Mama or Dada as a separate person.

Introducing your child to the world of books and the amazing stories and facts in them is a smart move. It naturally leads to education, laying a foundation for your child to develop a thirst for knowledge.

To create a voracious reader who engages happily with learning, such activity has to be fun. For my grandson, Conner, researching sea creatures and planets was fascinating. It wasn't work to soak in such information or to watch PBS specials on the sea and astronomy. He delighted in watching them with his ol' grandpa.

> Children are naturally curious, and parents and teachers can take full advantage of that with a smile.

The best kind of learning for young children is non-pressured. Children are naturally curious, and parents and teachers can take full advantage of that with a smile.

With preschool and kindergarten, the best schools combine understanding of young children and compassion for them. They use a lot of physical movement. Their programs balance age-appropriate learning with loving discipline. And fun is always an integral part of the curriculum.

Your Child's First School Experience

A child's first experience with school of any kind is very important. That's why I'm an advocate of preschool, as long as it's in a fun, interactive, learning environment. Preschool ought to be the time when kids go two to three times a week for two to three hours a day. Notice that I didn't say "all day" or "every day of the week."

However, for many families with both Mom and Dad working outside the home, the child goes to preschool in the morning and stays there for aftercare. But think through that strategy carefully before you do it. If you have a child who is dropped off at school at 7:00 a.m. and not picked up until 5:00 or 6:00 at night, that's way too long for a child that age to be in a learning environment. If you pulled a 10- or 11-hour shift at work five days a week, would you really like your work? Well, your child won't like school either.

Preschool children are too little to be gone from home that much. They tire out. Yes, there are naps and snacks and lots of playtime, but it's a very long day. Even if your child was at Disney World, that much stimulation is too much.

Your child's introduction to education needs to be done in a positive way, with a strong element of fun, and for just a few hours at a time. Two or three hours a day is perfect and enough, especially for a 3-year-old. Then they need to go home to their own environment so they can nap, rest, and play in a relaxed setting. Being home with Mom or Dad is the best option. Grandma or Grandpa is second.

> **Your child's introduction to education needs to be done in a positive way, with a strong element of fun, and for just a few hours at a time.**

In other words, if you need to work but have options available other than your child spending 11 hours in a pre-K setting, take them. Do some of your work at home, if possible. Or form a parent co-op with like-minded parents, where you switch off watching each other's kids for short periods. But make sure the group stays small (two to four kids, if possible) so it isn't just a replacement for the busy environment of pre-K. Every child deserves quiet time to rest and dream.

Because of a 3- to 5-year-old's developmental stage, let me encourage you not to think of preschool as a "holding place" for your child while you work. Whatever you choose for preschool needs to fit the needs, personality, and gifts of your child.

Take these two only children, for instance, whose moms chose very different options for pre-K schooling.

Adrian had a very musical and artistic bent. Instead of sending him to a regular preschool, his mom decided instead to do something innovative. She enrolled him in two young-child classes at their local college. One was every Monday and Wednesday morning for two hours and explored different art forms, such as texture painting and working with Play-Doh. The other was a music class for two hours every Tuesday and Thursday morning, where he could experiment with beginning instrument sounds and learn various rhythms. Mom worked Monday through Thursday mornings while Adrian was in class.

Shannon's mom chose a preschool nearby that offered a two-day option of three hours a day. Shannon was a smart little girl but tended to stay to herself. She clearly felt more comfortable around adults and older kids—very typical of only children. Her mom wanted to encourage her to interact with other children her own age. It was a tough transition for this stay-at-home mother and daughter, but they stuck with it. A month into preschool, Shannon's mom was finally smiling. She'd arrived to see her daughter skipping hand in hand with another girl. Shannon had at last made a friend.

Letting go of your child and having them move away from your influence to another location is extremely difficult for some parents, especially moms. At times, it's a necessity because the parents must work. But either way, broadening your child's experience by helping them learn certain skills such as sharing, communication, and following instructions is a good thing in the long term.

Preschool Readiness

The following skills are just basic guidelines. Depending on the age of the child (3 to 5 in pre-K), there is a wide difference in skill level. For some children, these skills may already have been perfected while others are just being introduced, especially in the 3-year-old classroom. A lot of readiness for preschool depends more on a child's personality than on their academic abilities.

Social readiness

- Is your child interested in going to school? Is she excited about the idea?
- Is he able to separate from you for a few hours to play with a friend?
- Does he know how to say "please" and "thank you," ask for help, and greet someone politely?
- Is her speech understandable and appropriate in volume and tone to be socially accepted by others?
- Is he able to play by himself for a period of time?
- Is she comfortable interacting with peers in groups?

Skill readiness

- Can he follow schedules? Remember two or three steps in sequence?
- Does she know what "day," "night," "morning," and "afternoon" mean?
- Does she pretend play to imitate life events (playing house, wedding, etc.)?
- Is he interested in animals? Does he know the different sounds they make, and can he imitate those sounds?
- Is she comfortable exploring the natural world (water, grass, etc.)?

WHAT WE DID

Jason is our fourth child. When he was 3, my husband's company downsized. Brad was able to keep his job, but at a reduced salary. Three of our kids were already in school full-time, but Jason was still home with me. He's our baby, and frankly, I wasn't ready to give him up. But I had to go back to work to help make our family finances work.

We enrolled Jason in a preschool that's close to my work. After a week, the administrator said Jason wasn't ready for pre-K. He would cry every time I left and would refuse to play with the other kids. But the school agreed to try to work with him.

A week later I got a call at work. Jason had started screaming and throwing things and hit one of the other kids. That child's parent threatened to sue the school and us. They insisted Jason be removed immediately from the environment.

That was a rough day, because I got docked in pay for leaving work, and we didn't know what we'd do with Jason the next day. I took two days of vacation that I hadn't even technically earned yet. Then, after brainstorming, Brad and I got a bright idea.

Jason had always loved playing with the little boy next door, and his mom stayed at home full-time. Now the boys could play together every morning while I was at work, and we moms would switch off making them lunch. Sometimes Brad and I paid our neighbor a small amount for helping out; other times I watched her son in the afternoon so she could run errands or have a break.

Because Jason got some needed social time—away from his brother and sister but with another child—he was more than ready for pre-K the following year. We put him in a different preschool, where he'd have a fresh start, and he loved it. This time it was a good match.

It was worth the creative brainstorming and the wait to get a win-win situation for all.

- Is she curious about how things work?
- Can he roughly match objects, whether by color or shape?
- Does she know a few colors?
- Can he grasp a pencil or stylus with his fingers rather than his fist?
- Does she make scribbles and tell you they're her name?
- Can he draw simple images with crayons or pencils? Explain what he's drawing?
- Does she know the first letter of her name?
- Can he tell a simple story? Identify main characters of a story? Sit still long enough for someone to read him a story?
- Does she know and identify the numbers 1, 2, and 3? Can she count with help?
- Is he able to hold a book himself and turn the pages?

Preschools often have their own readiness charts that are much more specific, so feel free to ask any you're evaluating for a checklist. Most pre-K children are 3 to 4 years old. Some preschools have early 5-year-olds and late 5-year-olds. But let me stress that every child's development in ages 3 to 5 is different. The above lists are meant to give you an idea, not be a strict measuring stick, for whether your child is ready in general for a preschool experience.

Kindergarten Readiness

Parents today tend to want their children in kindergarten early. If their child is three weeks short of the age cut-off deadline for kindergarten, usually parents push the school to admit their child. If there's more of a gap, the child may need to be voted on by the school board or go through additional assessments regarding readiness.

However, if the child is younger than the requirement, I always advise the parents to hold them back—especially if the child is a boy. Boys grow up more slowly than girls. Since physical prowess, strength, and size are important in the competitive world of males, holding a boy back will give him a needed edge. Instead of being the youngest and perhaps the smallest and weakest in the class of boys, he'll be one of the older and larger ones in the next kindergarten class.

How do you know if your child is ready for kindergarten?

Parents tend to think their child is a genius, so he must be ready for school. But your child needs to be prepared for kindergarten in three main ways.

Mentally

- Does your child listen to simple directions and follow them? Can she do what she's told?
- Can he stick with a task for a specific period of time? Does he stay on focus and have a good attention span?

- Can he tell you something that happened in sequential order?
- Does she recognize words that rhyme and/or begin with the same sound?
- Is she starting to write numbers and letters?
- Does he show an interest in learning? Is he intrigued by new information that's presented?
- Can he notice differences in pictures, shapes, and the sounds of words?
- Does she know the numbers 1 through 10, even if she says them out of order?
- Does she pretend to "read" a book by telling a story she makes up?

Physically

- Is she able to sit in her seat for the required lesson time? (Your child doesn't need to be able to sit for three hours in a row, but if she can't remain quietly in one spot long enough to listen to a story being read, then she's not ready for kindergarten.)
- Is he able to perform certain tasks, such as tying his own shoes?
- Does your child know when he has to go to the restroom, and can he manage that activity by himself? (If your child is in diapers, he is not ready for kindergarten, and most kindergartens won't allow him to enroll.)
- Is he able to complete basic fine motor skills, such as holding scissors and a pencil or stylus?

- Can she draw a self-portrait with a head and body, arms and legs, a basic face, and hands and feet?
- Is she able to participate in gross motor skills, such as throwing a ball, running, and jumping?

Socially

- Is he mature enough to handle social situations in a larger group?
- Can she play well with others? Get along with peers?
- Can she let others have their turn in the spotlight?
- Can he share, cooperate, and take turns? (This skill usually needs continued development with most young children.)
- Can she handle her emotions? Does she have self-control and know what to do when she gets upset? Has she developed coping strategies acceptable to a classroom setting? (It's normal for kindergarten children to cry when they're upset. But if they throw things as their coping mechanism, that's not an acceptable response.)

To enter kindergarten, your child doesn't have to be able to do all of these things well. However, if you hesitate to say yes to many of these questions, then your child may be better off with another year of pre-K first. Many kids aren't ready for kindergarten by age 5. If your child isn't, then delay his start. It really is the best thing in the long run.

If you have twins, one might be ready and the other might not be. Just because they're twins doesn't mean they have the same personality. From babyhood, one might have eyes wide open when they're supposed to be shut, and be saying, "Where's the party?" at 30 days of age. The other might be like a manatee, sunning herself in a quiet environment. Even if they both are ready for kindergarten, it's probably best if they are at least in a different class, with a different teacher who won't compare them.

If you have any doubt if your child is ready for kindergarten, hold him back a year. Give him that extra time to allow him to succeed in the competitive school environment. Today's kindergarten is more like what first grade was for you—at least that's what many parents say. There is increased academic pressure, more testing, and more competition. Peer pressure is also a significant factor.

In addition, reread all the preschool readiness information regarding different subjects. How is your child doing in those areas? There's a difference between *meeting* and *exceeding* expectations. You don't want a child to be overwhelmed by not being prepared for the basics of kindergarten. But you don't want him to be bored by the tasks of kindergarten either. If he is, he'll turn off his attention and won't desire to excel in the classroom.

Some kids are later bloomers. Others aren't ready for the stress and structure of a kindergarten environment. They need that extra year to become ready. The years you have your child at home fly by quickly, so what's the rush?

Evaluating the Education Environment

As you check out local preschool and kindergarten options, don't just evaluate the school. Meet the teachers and principal. Are they flexible and friendly? Do they look at each child as a unique creature or as merely one of the crowd they're responsible for?

A smart and experienced teacher assesses her students as they walk through the door on the first day. Sarah, who has taught kindergarten for 12 years, told me she watched from the curb as little Cayden exited his mother's car and then swung his backpack freely from side to side. Where it landed, he didn't care, even when it whacked another child in the head.

Little Hannah arrived next. If a kindergarten aide hadn't taken her by the hand and steered her back to the sidewalk, she would have wandered willy-nilly in the dirt nearby, trampling the flowers.

Those two weren't the only nomads in Sarah's class either. She swiftly realized she had an entire classroom of children who were all about movement. They would need to move in order to learn. They had no idea what it meant to sit down, pay attention, or focus their eyes up front. So she adapted her teaching style to incorporate lots of movement throughout the day, including little trips to walk around the grounds of the school and explore.

If flexibility, adaptation, and fun are part of their first academic experience, your children are primed to start off on the right foot with education. Experienced teachers and wise parents know what's most important for children who are starting off in school—that they have a pleasurable, exhilarating experience. But they also need to be mature enough and prepared to take on whatever lies in front of them mentally, emotionally, physically, and socially on the educational journey. The more excited your child is about school—if he's not holding back and fearful of the change—the easier the transition will be for you, him, and his teacher.

Your role as a parent is to make the most informed choice you can for your child, based on your unique knowledge of him, his readiness, and the pre-K or kindergarten's policies. If you think your child is ready for the challenge, go for it! If it ends up being more than you bargained for and your child needs extra time, there's nothing wrong with repeating pre-K or kindergarten. We did that with one of our own kids who wasn't quite ready for the next schooling step. Today she's living proof that we did the right thing. She's flying high in every way in her career, life, and relationships.

7

Homework and Grades

*What homework and grades really mean, and
how best to motivate your child.*

You roll your eyes. The nightly fracas is already starting. As soon as the homework comes out of the backpack, the stress ratchets up between you and your child. You can predict what will happen—the tears, the yelling, the slam and click of the bedroom door. You both go to bed angry, and you feel guilty. *What am I doing wrong as a parent? Why is this like a continual replay of a bad movie?*

And nothing can kick up more hullabaloo in the kitchen than report cards arriving . . . and not being quite what you expected. There the truth is, in black and white, of exactly what your kid *didn't* do for the quarter or semester.

But stop right there. How important are homework and grades? What do they really mean, and how much should

154

you push? If your system of reward and punishment isn't working, this chapter will help.

Homework—Whose Is It?

When it comes to homework, children usually fall into one of four categories.

The manipulator

"Can you help me? This is so hard!" 10-year-old Brittney pleads with you.

You fall for her big, blue, innocent-looking eyes once again. You sit down with your daughter at her desk and "help" her with math. But after 20 minutes, she gives you "the look." The disgusted "I hate you, and it's all your fault" look.

"I just don't understand it!" she says, and tears well up.

"Honey, you just told me 4 × 5 = 20. Now you're telling me 5 × 5 = 15. Does that make any sense?" you ask.

Now you get the full waterworks. "You don't understand. You never understand me!" she wails.

Parent, don't fall for it. That kid is working you. All she wants to know is the answer. She isn't pulling her weight in learning. The only thing she's learning is how to manipulate you into feeling bad for her so you fill in the blanks. So who really is doing her homework?

Stop right there. Put that pen or stylus down. Say, "Honey, this doesn't seem to be working. You aren't trying to understand. I can't help you any further." Then walk out of the room. Don't own what isn't yours. Her fifth-grade math homework isn't your assignment. If she's struggling that badly, she can ask her teacher for help the next day. If that still doesn't do the trick, and the teacher relates to you that your child is behind in her skills, perhaps it's time to get an after-school tutor.

Her art project that she should have started three weeks ago and is due in two days isn't your homework either. Chances are that when she finally does it, it'll look like it was put together in two days. But don't rescue her.

> **Some kids need to stop manipulating others to do their work and start doing the work themselves.**

Is there a lesson in this for your child? When you decide to stop snowplowing her road in life?

Some kids need to stop manipulating others to do their work and start doing the work themselves. No, work isn't always easy. That's why it's called *work*. But it's something we all have to get used to. The sooner, the better.

The unorganized

Matt's work area in his bedroom looked a lot like Pig-Pen in the Peanuts cartoon, his mom told me.

"It's such a mess, I have no idea where he can find anything. He just throws everything in a pile. No wonder he can't get his homework done on time. He never knows what's due when."

Some kids are fully capable of doing their homework. They just need a little assistance initially in organizing their work and schedule. Note I said *initially*. That doesn't mean you organize him for the entire school year. Once the system is set up, helping him out for a few days is one thing. Helping him for an entire semester is another. So if beef jerky, smelly sweat socks, books, folders, and a smashed cupcake are falling simultaneously out of your child's backpack after school, and his work space is completely disorganized, you would do well to step in and suggest some organization.

A lot of kids, when going into junior high especially, are faced for the first time with multiple teachers of multiple subjects. The amount of information and expectations can be overwhelming to children who aren't naturally organized.

The best suggestion I've come across is making a hanging file folder for each subject and labeling it with the subject matter. Even better if each subject is a different color. Put the folders in a drawer or a box that's kept in your kitchen or family room. When your child comes home, he dumps out the backpack as soon as he walks in the door (even before he hits the fridge and snack cabinet) and stashes each assignment in the appropriate folder. Then when he's ready for homework, he's not wading through the complete mess in his backpack. He just picks up one folder at a time and takes it to where he does homework. That simple tip has calmed the homework waters for many families I know.

> Some kids are fully capable of doing their homework. They just need a little assistance initially in organizing their work and schedule.

Many kids just need a leg up structure-wise, since they haven't encountered mass organization before. Then they can handle the rest on their own.

If he needs more structure for projects that are long-range, clip a note to the folder, such as, "Science project due in two weeks." Have your child also list the steps he needs to do for the experiment and when they're due. That way, when he picks up the science folder each night to check for homework, he won't miss an important step that has to get done that day, because the reminder is there.

And guess what? You didn't even have to nag. What a bonus!

The overstructured perfectionist

It was a common scene in the Walkers' home—11-year-old Brandon going a little nuts because his math homework wasn't precisely where he'd put it the night before. But in a family of four active younger kids, things rarely remained in the same location.

> Perfectionists are the young kids who use erasers so much that they wear a hole in their homework.

Brandon, a perfectionist, followed a rigorous schedule he'd set up for himself. That included wearing his favorite shirt every Wednesday. If it was in the wash, look out, world. Brandon became a force to be reckoned with that rivaled Darth Vader.

Some kids are intrigued by schedules and details, but they're also controlled by them. Perfectionists are the young kids who use erasers so much that they wear a hole in their homework. They'll melt down right in front of you if something doesn't turn out the way they'd envisioned.

With such kids, it's time for a teachable moment. Put your hand on your child's arm and say, "Honey, I know this is a huge deal for you. I can see that by the look on your face. But I'll tell you the truth—this isn't a big thing to me." Then turn your back and walk away.

Why do that? Because your child is having that meltdown for one reason—to engage you in battle since his life isn't perfect. Such action on your part ends the drama. You state the truth simply, but you don't pay off his perfectionistic behavior by belaboring the facts with undue attention or sticking around for more of his tantrum-throwing show.

Your child may not be calm enough to see reason right now, but later he'll think about your words. I guarantee it, especially since he's a detailed-oriented kid. He'll recall every single thing you said and examine it from all angles.

The balancer

This is the child every parent longs to have. She is self-motivated, so you've never once had to tell her to study in her entire academic career. She's organized and on top of her schedule. In fact, she's likely to be the one to remind you where you need to be on her behalf, whether it's a parent-teacher meeting or a school event. When she brings home her report card, she leaves it confidently on the counter but doesn't make a big deal about it. She knows she's done well, so she's not worried.

> If you have this kind of child, you truly have one in a million, and you better thank your lucky stars every day. Numerous parents would like to clone your kid and transport her into their own homes.

Because she's internally motivated by her own desires and dreams, a report card is a mere blip on the screen for her. It's something she looks at for a second before she moves on with her next plans in life. She doesn't focus on anything that's in the past, because she's a forward thinker and an achiever.

If you have this kind of child, you truly have one in a million, and you better thank your lucky stars every day. Numerous parents would like to clone your kid and transport her into their own homes.

I have a friend who has a daughter like that. She has excelled in nearly every area since she learned to walk. I can't wait to see how high that girl, now a teenager, will fly someday in her adult years with her confident, world-changing personality and finely honed skills.

But even children who are confident and excellent in their craft still need parental approval and affirmation. So when you see that report card on the counter, open it and bask in the parental "Ahh" for a minute. Then pop into her room with the report card in hand.

"Wow, amazing," you say as she looks up from the homework she's already plunged into on her Chromebook. "I'm such a lucky mom to get to see you develop wonderfully in so many areas. I get to see these awesome grades, and so do others. But grades are only one part of the picture. They don't make you who you are."

You smile. "I love being able to see all sides of you as you discover more about the world. You already know who you are, and I love seeing you explore your many talents. Your confidence and risk-taking spirit will take you up and over any failures and hurdles you might face. I'm so glad you enjoy learning, and I can't wait to see what you pursue in the future. You'll always be my girl."

Those simple but heartfelt words will be the cherry on top of her already strong internal motivation. You can bet that kid will keep powering on.

How to *Really* Help Your Child with Homework

Not telling your kids what to do is a new art form for parents, because telling them what to do is a natural response when you're an authority figure. Instead, by not taking ownership of things and events that aren't yours, you provide opportunities for your kids to make decisions that either work or fail in regard to their homework and grades.

> Not telling your kids what to do is a new art form for parents, because telling them what to do is a natural response.

So, what should your roles in homework be?

First, *provide a low-noise area of your house where your kids can do homework.* Yes, today's kids are multi-taskers who will tend to do homework, text their friends, and listen to music simultaneously. Some are efficient at it, and it works. For others, trying to do all three is a recipe for disaster academically.

Learning what works best for your child can only come through trial and error. But you can start by making sure your child has a quiet area to work in. If he shares a room with a sibling, that can get tricky, but you can institute "quiet hours" for studying, or have one of the siblings use a corner of the family room while the other uses the bedroom.

Second, *keep an eye on when and how they're getting their homework done, but don't interfere unless you see a*

161

pattern of them not doing it or frustration taking over. Kids will usually find their own schedules after some trial and error. Some want to do it as soon as they're home and get it over with. Others want playtime first, then will start on homework after dinner. Your night-owl teenager may not start it until 10:00 p.m., after her social activities are over.

As soon as your babies enter your family, you can see that they are different. They look different, act differently, and have their own schedules. That's why you should treat them differently. You quickly learn the habits of each of your children. You can tell by the little fists rubbing their eyes or other body language when it's time to lay that kid down for a nap.

In the same way, if your kids are studying, you instinctively know when they need a snack, a word of encouragement, or a "Hey, let's take a little break" when they're getting frustrated. It's not the end of the world to close a book and not look at it until the next day. Sometimes a fresh perspective is just what the doctor ordered.

It's certainly a lot better than you saying, "Give it to me and I'll finish it up. You go to sleep." That's not teaching your child responsibility or accountability regarding work.

As the parent, you are always walking on a balance beam. You've got the answers in your back pocket since you've walked that beam before. But it's your child's first time trying that balancing act. Sometimes she'll fall off and have to get back on. That's part of her academic journey and of life in general.

Third, *be available when needed.* Sometimes your child needs someone to quiz him on math flash cards. Other times he may need you to be the audience as he practices his speech.

What's important is that you always make time for your choice and that he knows he's a priority.

You should never do the work *for* him. You've done your time at school. Yes, it may have felt like the county jail to you at times. But if you play your cards right in choosing the best schooling option for your child, it doesn't have to feel like that to him.

What Grades Really Mean

Grades don't have as much meaning as we sometimes give them, especially when a child is young and settling in to the concept of school. However, they are important in helping you, teachers, and administration figure out if your child is performing to the expectations of a grade level.

The Every Student Succeeds Act (ESSA), signed into law at the end of 2015, is well known to every educator. What does it mean? That every child—no matter what race, income, background, or home situation—deserves the opportunity to be educated so they can make of themselves what they want to be. It was signed into being when the No Child Left Behind (NCLB) Act, a previous version of the law, expired. It means every child deserves educational opportunities suited to them.

Will every child be equal in gifts, intelligence, and opportunities? No. The only way for schools to know if a child is successfully learning information at their age-appropriate level is through testing. To pass from one grade level to another, you have to achieve a test score within a certain range. The key of ESSA education is to see growth in students from point A in August to point B in May or June.

163

As younger kids settle in to school, their grades can fluctuate greatly as they learn how to study and process information. Grades can also change as their maturity level changes, giving them the ability to focus for longer periods of time.

For older kids, especially those going into high school, cumulative quarter or semester grades become more important. Someday a person your child doesn't know will look at a computer screen that has basic information about your child on it, including grades, test scores, and written references from counselors and teachers. That person, part of the undergraduate admissions department of a college or university, will make judgments about your child in an empirical fashion based on that information. Yes, you might think your son is brilliant. But he won't come off that way to a third party if he's getting Cs in every subject and even fails PE.

How to Handle Unsatisfactory Report Cards

One bad report card isn't the end of the world, like many parents make it out to be. However, it is like waving a cautionary flag in a road race. It should get your attention.

Don't overreact, but take action.

When you talk with a child about an unsatisfactory report card, don't overreact. "Oh my goodness! You never told me you were struggling so much. Cs and Ds? I know you're smarter than that. What's wrong with you?"

It's better to say, "Wow, Cs and Ds. My guess is that you're not too happy with this report card, because you know you could have done better."

164

"Yeah, Dad," your son replies. "I'll just study harder next time."

You nod. "That's good. Then let me help you. For this next semester, in order to allow you to have more time to concentrate, let's put a hold on your job at the store."

"But Dad," he argues, "I have to save so I can get a car. You know I've been working hard on that."

You're smart enough not to get dragged into that battle, because you know the argument will only escalate and you'll both be losers. "That's a great goal," you say, "and I'm sure you'll get there. But right now your main job is to be a student. We're not taking your job away—there's no punishment here. I know you work hard at it. But let's just try putting a hold on it for a few months so you have more time to focus on your studies. Your uncle Bob will understand."

> One bad report card isn't the end of the world. However, it is like waving a cautionary flag in a road race. It should get your attention.

By doing this, you're saying, "We value education and your performance in the classroom. They're important."

You've just taken your clippers out and gone after your son's wings by curtailing his part-time job. He's smart enough to read between the lines. *I better try harder to study or it'll take me a really long time to get that car.* His motivation kicks into high gear.

If your child can't keep up with school expectations, then it's time to limit one or more extracurricular activities to get him on track. If you do so, you'll swiftly figure out if he can do the work but hasn't been motivated to, or whether he's unable to do that level of work and needs some assistance.

You might think it's a bit harsh to limit his activities. But you're really following the course of what the school itself would do. Let's say your child doesn't work to maintain a good enough grade average to play football. What happens? He doesn't play football.

That's reality at school. It should be that way in your home too. B doesn't happen until A is completed. That little bit of reality discipline is as clear as day. No room for your child to wiggle out of it.

Keep in mind whose grades they are.

Sometimes the best and most honest answer to a lousy report card is, "Honey, I'm sorry you don't like learning. Even some effort could have gotten you Cs. This report card . . . well, it's unacceptable. It shows that you haven't put forward any effort. We both know you're much more capable than this piece of paper shows. And there's something else I want you to notice. My name isn't on your report card. Yours is. These are your grades."

Bryce tries to sidetrack you by retorting, "But I don't like my teacher. She's mean."

You say calmly, "From day one on this earth, people have always made excuses. Adam, the first human being, sure did. God told him directly not to eat of the fruit from a certain tree in the garden, but he did anyway. When God confronted him with what he did, Adam flung these words back in God's face: 'It was the woman you gave me who made me do it.'

"Honey, it's always tempting to try to pass the buck. To blame the teacher or someone else. But this report card? These grades? They're yours and yours alone. One of the things I really love and appreciate about you is that most of the time you pony up. When you blow it, you say, 'Hey, it's my fault. I could have done better.' I think this is one of those times you should consider doing that. That's all I'm saying."

Then you turn your back and walk away.

Notice that you aren't lambasting the kid, saying he's stupid. You aren't lecturing him about everything he did wrong. You're just tossing the ball of responsibility back into his court, where it belongs. You're saying one of the traits you appreciate about him is his honesty. Then you leave him to reflect on your words.

No pointed fingers.

No raised voice.

No last-minute ballistic missile lobbed in his direction.

You just walk away calmly.

I guarantee that with such an approach, guilt will set in to your child's psyche very swiftly. He will temporarily be unhappy, and with good reason. He let the ball drop on his side of the net.

Let your child stew in that guilt for a while. Guilt isn't always a bad thing, as it's often portrayed to be. It can be good if it pushes your child past his failure and gets his eye back on the ball in the game.

Hey, Mom's right, Bryce thinks as he sits on his bed. *I really didn't try. I just threw together those papers and didn't study much for the finals. I admit, those grades are pretty bad.*

Then the fact that you weren't condescending or angry sinks in. *Still, Mom didn't say I was dumb. She knows I can do better.*

Next, resolve sets in. *Okay, so I'll do better. I'll show her and everybody else just what I can do.*

Congratulations. Your child has just taken ownership of his grades.

Good thing too. Because they're not yours, they're his.

Keep in mind the age of your child.

How you handle the aftereffects of unsatisfactory grades has a lot to do with the age of your child. If your child is younger, go for more of the direct approach. Find practical ways to help.

"Honey, after dinner tonight, you and I are going to play a game. We'll have a contest to see who can get the most multiplication facts right within a certain period of time."

Of course, you'll have to let your child win some points, especially if you're a tax accountant. Your end game is to spend time going over the multiplication tables, because clearly your child doesn't know them and can't proceed forward in math until she does.

> You can lead your "horse" to water, but you can't make him drink. Only he can do that.

With older kids—middle school and up—curtailing their wings is more indirect. The motivation comes through your conversation and a rearranging of their priorities that makes the kid realize, *Uh-oh, unless I start doing better, these bad grades are going to affect my social life or my ability to play hockey, shoot baskets, or get my driver's license.*

Let me be clear. You can lead your "horse" to water, but you can't make him drink. Only he can do that.

Will your first efforts instantly be successful? Maybe. Maybe not. Your child may be stubborn and dug in. If you have one with that type of personality and all else fails, employ what I call "the bread and water treatment." All other activities and privileges go away until the child gets serious about studying.

Yes, it may sound prison-like and cruel, especially if Grandma gets wind of it, but you're after the long game.

A Word to the Wise

If you look at your child's report card and see he's doing well, you ought to be tremendously happy. I know some parents who would pray for even one C!

Instead of just accepting good grades as "the usual fare," make sure you acknowledge the hard work they represent. Noticing that achievement and commenting on it verbally have a profound effect on your child.

"That's a wonderful report card. And you know what's so wonderful about it?" You smile broadly. "It captures in just a few letters all the hard work, determination, and diligence you've put into this last period of school. Wow, you brought two of those marks up a full letter grade. I've seen you working in your room late at night. Congratulations on a job well done."

Your son will walk away with warmth in his heart and a spring in his step because you noticed his hard work. Your encouraging words are his reward for his perseverance and all the nights he studied instead of playing on his Xbox.

If you're one of those parents who looks at your child's report card full of As and spots the one A minus first, there's a clinical term for you—you're *nuts*. You should call my office ASAP and make an appointment for yourself because you've got serious problems. With a report card like that, are you really going to pick on the one grade that has a little minus mark after it? If you do, you'll kick off a war with your child, because she knows she can never perform well enough for you.

If you're one of those people who has a PhD in flaw picking—who zeroes in on anything that's slightly negative—the best thing you can do for yourself and those around you is learn how to respond instead of react. That means you keep your mouth shut until you can think through what you'd normally say and do. "You got an A minus in history? I graduated from military academy, and your grandpa was a history teacher. I know you can do better than that," you may tell your daughter.

If she's a pleaser, she will deflate visibly in front of your eyes. If she's got spunk, that "ready to fight" light will glint in her eyes. She'll be more than capable of dragging you into a battle.

Here's where you as a parent need to see that flashing caution light. If you don't stop and pay heed, you'll get sucked into a place you don't want to go.

Do you really want the kind of relationship with your child where the only words you can exchange are fighting, hurtful ones? Where anything you say to each other escalates? Or do you want to exert some self-control, screech to a halt right now, and do something different?

Let's replay that scene. This time, focus on all those blindingly wonderful As. After all, even an A minus is an A. Then say, "This report card is amazing, honey. You work so hard. You must be so happy with yourself at seeing these results, and deservedly so. Getting these kinds of grades says so much about your determination to do well in life. I know some of the papers and tests were really difficult for you—your mom told me that—but we believe in you. You're going to go amazing places in life."

Now your daughter is looking at you with amazed eyes. You've not only surprised her, but you've won her heart.

You see, if you're a flaw picker, you've paid for that critical nature in lots of ways. I bet you pay for it at work (I'm sure co-workers don't appreciate it). You've certainly paid for it in your marriage and in any relationship, including the one with your daughter. The good news is, it's not too late to turn your flaw picking around and pursue the parent-child relationship you want to have.

You just need to follow the rules you learned in kindergarten before crossing a street: *Stop. Look. Listen.* If you do a little internal self-talk before you open your mouth, you can choose your response rather than reacting the way you usually would.

Stop. Ask yourself, *What would I normally say or do when I see my kid's report card?*

> **If you do a little internal self-talk before you open your mouth, you can choose your response rather than reacting the way you usually would.**

Look. Ask yourself, *What does that report card really reveal? What am I going to do and say differently to change the outcome of our usual exchanges?*

Listen. Take a look at your daughter's face. More than anything else, she desires your approval. Will you listen to what her heart is saying—*Dad, do you love me? Even with that A minus?*—and respond appropriately in a way that grows your relationship?

Yes, you've been trained since childhood to react nega-tively, most likely because you had one parent or—heaven help you—*two* parents who were also flaw pickers. The good news is, you're not too old to learn a few new tricks. Yes, it'll take some hard work to reorient your automatic responses. But you are capable of relearning that behavior. I know it.

Most of all, everyone in your life will be thankful for your efforts.

A New Perspective on Failure

So many parents hold the view that failure is bad. It isn't an option for them—and certainly isn't for their child. But I want you to think for a minute. What people do you really admire who are very successful in what they do?

Think about or research their backgrounds. Chances are, those people have failed miserably in some area of life. But you know what? That failure led them to success. Why? Because they decided that they wouldn't lie there wallowing in the mud. Instead, they got up, cleaned themselves off, and chose to do something differently. Each time they did that, they confirmed their resolve not to give up until they reached their dreams.

Failure, in my view, is necessary for success. That's why one of the questions many prestigious universities such as Stanford ask prospective students is, "When have you failed, how did you deal with it, and how has that failure influenced your path in life?"

To know success, you have to experience failure and push on from there.

Some kids fall apart when they fail or make mistakes. When Abigail brought home her first C in sixth grade, she angrily flung at her mother, "I want to quit school! I'm never going back!" then dissolved into tears.

Christie was surprised not only at the grade but at her daughter's behavior. Abigail had never cried over a grade before. Then again, schoolwork had always been easy for her daughter. Since she'd entered middle school, though, the work had been a lot harder.

Christie put a gentle hand on her sobbing daughter's back. "Honey, I know this is a huge thing to you. But I also know you gave it your best shot, like you always do. This

To know success, you have to experience failure and push on from there.

really isn't a big deal to me. It's only a little ripple in life, and there will be more ripples to come. I believe in you. You'll be able to handle this situation after you have time to think it through. If you need some quiet time to do so, I understand."

That mom didn't allow herself to get dragged into a battle merely because her daughter was emotional over feeling like a failure. Christie merely stated the facts, highlighted that what happened wasn't a big deal, and assured her daughter that she could handle it. In short, she gave her daughter permission to move on in life.

Now that's a smart mom who knows that homework and grades come and go. But what's truly important and lasting is her relationship with her child.

Failure has to be acceptable within your home. It has to be framed in a proper perspective. If you don't allow your child to fail within the safe environment of your home, she'll become the kind of child who sticks a toe in the water of new experiences but refuses to wade in farther.

Whenever I see a child who is reticent to try new things, I know it's most likely because he has a parent who is always "shoulding" on him at home. If you constantly convey to your child that he should be doing better with grades and homework, he'll swiftly start tuning you out. What he hears you saying with your pestering is, "I don't like who you are now." What he's saying by tuning out is, "I'm not going to be who you want me to be."

And the silent war ensues.

If you're a flaw picker and you're dealing with a firstborn or only child, you're treading on particularly dangerous waters. Firstborns and onlies already have strong perfectionistic streaks. They're their own worst enemies. You don't need to add to the stress by pointing out any flaws. Those are already magnified by their birth order traits.

When a parent brings me a firstborn or only child who procrastinates in doing his homework or "isn't living up to his full potential," the first thing I take a look at is the parent's behavior. If the parent is critical, the kid has basically given up. He isn't doing homework out of fear that he'll be wrong on an answer. With his personality type, he'd rather not complete the work than be labeled *wrong*. That's because firstborns and onlies greatly fear judgment and bad evaluations from people in authority.

Any reward and punishment techniques you try will never work on your kid if you continue to have a critical eye. Your child will never bloom into the flower she can be if you're constantly hovering over her, watching for the least little sprout to rear its head out of the soil. You'd do better to

WHAT WE DID

When I was growing up, my parents paid my brothers and me to get good grades. An A was worth $20, a B $10, and a C $2, but Ds and Fs got nothing. We tended to work hard to get good grades, since extra money was tough to come by in our family. My dad also impressed on us the value of a college education, and we wanted good grades for our transcript.

I tried the same motivation with my daughter, but it didn't work. I know she's smart, but she consistently got Cs. She didn't study for tests and gave her homework only passing attention. Her freshman year of high school, we decided we needed to find a new motivation. So I did what my parents never did for me. I went to Cassie and asked her what would motivate her.

At first she looked puzzled. Then she said, "I really want to become a fashion designer."

When I thought about it, that made sense. She's always been creative with crafts and clothing. So I said, "Okay. What do you think it'll take to get you there?"

We started researching together to see what schools focused on fashion design and what their application process was. The lightbulb went on in my daughter's head. Good grades mattered for what she wanted to do in life.

From that night on, she was motivated. The next semester, she earned As and Bs and handed me her report card with a smile. She'd gained the best motivation of all—the satisfying internal motivation of heading toward her dream.

That motivation continued all the way through high school. Now she's a sophomore at a university. Guess what she's studying? Fashion design!

step away from your control and "shoulding" and allow your little sprout some fresh air to breathe.

Why Reward and Punishment Don't Work

Most of us grew up with a system of reward and punishment, and we're still trying to make it work on our kids. But did it really work on you?

Sure, Dad's wrath didn't rain down on your head any longer after you improved your report card. Your mom might even have slipped you a surprise or two for your hard work. But now that you have a job, does your supervisor reward you with a "good job" or a bonus every time you do your work? Then why are you setting up a system for your kids that won't work in real life?

> Why are you setting up a system for your kids that won't work in real life? It's like trying to reward a kid who is potty training with M&Ms. Do you get M&Ms every time you go potty?

It's like trying to reward a kid who is potty training with M&Ms. Do you get M&Ms every time you go potty?

Our tendency as parents is to build in all kinds of rewards for our kids. If they get an A, they'll get X bucks. If a B, it's this amount. If a C, well, that's a couple bucks. Get a D or F and they get the privilege of cleaning the toilets for a month.

Rewarding or punishing your children is never the healthiest option. What's best is that your kids learn that there's a direct connection between the work they do in the classroom, the homework they do and turn in, and the grades they receive. If they work hard, they're more likely to succeed in school and in life.

But what's even better is the feeling they get inside when they know they have performed well, to the best of their ability. If a teacher or parent says, "Wow, great job. The work you did really paid off," that's an additional stroke of encouragement for the internal motivation and good feeling that already exist.

Because external motivation relies on someone else, it can't follow your child through life. But internal motivation can. It will relentlessly drive your child to achieve his passions and dreams in ways that are beyond even your wildest expectations.

Just watch and see.

8

Top Traits of the Absolute Best Schools

How to know if you've found just what you're looking for.

Schools change. I'm sure there are public school districts in your town that used to be very good. Now they're not so good. Populations shift. A school that wasn't so good a few years ago is now a top magnet or vocational school. The homeschooling network that didn't exist even five years ago in your area is now a full-service organization that offers wonderful options. A charter school has popped up less than a mile from your neighborhood public school. The military academy that used to be higher priced now has an organizational donor who offers scholarships.

You can explore your options through brochures or websites, but there's no substitute for visiting the real thing.

What to Look For

How do you know if you've found just what you're looking for? The absolute best schools all share some top traits.

The school has a safe, clean, and organized environment.

First of all, the campus grounds and buildings must be safe. There is control over who can enter the campus. Not just anyone can walk in the front door of the building and be able to get to the students. Anyone visiting the school has to go into a reception area first, which is separated by electronic doors and perhaps a metal scanner. Everyone has to sign in, have a reason for visiting the campus, and wear an identity tag while there. In today's world of school shootings, safety is a primary concern for all schools and most parents' top concern.

No bullying or put-downs—whether physical, verbal, or via the internet—are tolerated. Hallways and restrooms are monitored. Everyone is treated respectfully. Infractions are swiftly handled with loving discipline.

The school interior and grounds are also clean and groomed. Classrooms are organized and attractive. Trash is picked up. Restrooms and floors are cleaned on a daily basis. The school campus is treated with respect by the students because they consider it "their place."

The school has a rigorous curriculum, with academic excellence and high expectations.

Programs are top-notch, are cutting-edge, and use today's technology. They're tough, not watered down to make students look good and parents happy with the grades. An A means nothing to a student long-term if it's not truly earned.

For students who attend the school, there is a built-in expectation that they will do the work to the best of their ability. No, they don't have to be the sharpest tool in the shed, but they do have to work their hardest. Though expectations are high, they are also age-appropriate, manageable, and motivating to each individual child. The point is to educate the child to the utmost of his or her ability in every area possible.

Some schools are complete systems—in other words, your child can start in kindergarten and go all the way through grade 12. Or the school might be K–5 or K–8. If a school covers all grades, you have the advantage of a continuing curriculum that builds year by year, rather than overlapping curriculum. For example, Jacob attended grades 1–8 in one school, then switched to a different school for grades 9–12. Because of overlapping curriculum, he studied the same content about World War II twice instead of being introduced to new content.

> **Though expectations are high, they are also age-appropriate, manageable, and motivating to each individual child.**

Kindergarten and first grade can also have some overlaps. Emily was surprised when her daughter's private kindergarten taught cursive instead of print for writing letters. It was an experiment the school curriculum director did for only one year, without it being explained to parents. When Emily's daughter changed schools after kindergarten, her first grade taught print and second grade taught cursive. Her young daughter was understandably a little confused, since she was the only one in the class who'd learned it "backwards," according to her new teacher.

Make sure you understand the curriculum the school uses, and how and when it's introduced to your child. The best schools have time-tested curriculum that is integrated from grade to grade, covers a spectrum of subjects, and follows a linear pattern of learning.

The school has a friendly, caring, respectful atmosphere based on accountability.

The atmosphere is based on the Golden Rule: treat others as you want to be treated. It is one of respect and accountability. It models the mantra, "We're all in this together." No one child is the center of the universe, and scholars don't compete against each other. Every individual scholar is part of a bigger unit of the school that works together.

When you visit the school, you are warmly welcomed and invited on a tour. Faculty and staff don't treat children simply as one of many in a line of indistinguishable faces; they greet children they pass by first name. The attitude of everyone you meet is personable. Their body language is friendly. People are treated with respect. The atmosphere that surrounds the school feels happy.

> If you don't feel a warmth and connection when you walk in the school door, imagine what it's going to be like for your child when you're not around.

As a result, you can see your child feeling comfortable going there. The smiles you encounter from the children you meet at school say it all: "We like being here. We feel special."

Keep in mind that in order for a school to be a school, it needs students. Many schools put their best foot forward for the adults who visit. If you don't feel a warmth and connection when you walk in the school door, imagine what it's going to be like for your child when you're not around.

Learning is fun and interactive.

Book learning is only one form of education. For younger children especially, hands-on learning is critical. Kids naturally enjoy learning unless it is pressured or the topic is boring. (Do you pay attention if someone speaking is boring? Your kids have the same yawn response.) The best schools believe that children need to be approached in the right way in an environment that is conducive to learning in order for them to soar.

The best schools don't merely "teach to the test" in order to earn a good rating. With Common Core curriculum, schools are graded by the state. They become A, B, C, or D schools as a result. Quality schools focus on true learning—where children not only absorb and recall subject matter but incorporate it into their lives and learn to be critical thinkers.

The environment also reveals the fun, interactive learning of the school. For example, student artwork adorns the walls to brighten the surroundings, and there are music fairs and game nights.

Teachers are certified, are experts in their field, and engage with students both one-on-one and in a group.

Teachers must be qualified, not simply be teaching a particular subject because there is no one else to do so. Many public school districts today, especially in large cities, don't have enough teachers to go around. One school district in Tucson had 100 vacancies midyear. So who was in the classroom? Aides, much of the time.

Good teachers at quality schools have the following characteristics:

- They are warm and nurturing, looking for ways to creatively and actively engage with and challenge students from diverse backgrounds.
- They use cutting-edge technology as a friend and mentor to teach academic skills and inspire learning.
- They welcome questions, differing viewpoints, and an exchange of ideas. They aren't the only ones doing the talking.
- They encourage critical, high-level thinking and dialogue in all areas.
- They motivate students to work independently or in small groups without a lot of direction.
- They make the classroom a fun, exciting, friendly, safe place to be.

Uniqueness is not only recognized but applauded.

Every child is treated as unique, with unique gifts and as a unique gift to humankind. The school goes out of their way to encourage talents, to use them to benefit the whole (such as allowing students to paint murals on a wall or to showcase their musical or athletic abilities), and to serve individual students. Exceptional scholars—a term I use for children who have special needs—are welcomed and incorporated into regular classrooms, with additional help where needed.

Encouragement reigns, and basic etiquette is expected.

The mantra of the school is, "Expect the best, and you'll get the best." Encouragement reigns and spreads like wildfire. Children, faculty, and staff all adhere to basic life courtesies. They say "please" and "thank you." They greet each other. They open the door for each other. Good manners and self-discipline are expected, taught, and followed as practical skills for every day.

In such a way, students prepare for life both inside and outside the classroom. Developing quality, respectful relationships is considered a key to schooling success. What you learn at school directly relates to life outside of school. Education and real life are integrated.

Relational discipline rather than punishment is taught.

Responsibility and accountability are important for the best schools to work well. Discipline doesn't consist of punishment but rather is relational. For example, if a child doesn't finish a homework assignment on time, he doesn't go anywhere else—including to his track meet—until that assignment is completed. The principle of "B doesn't happen until A is completed" reigns.

School policies are clearly defined regarding discipline, so there are no surprises. Teachers are backed by administration in their decisions. Parents are expected to be on board with teachers and administration in adhering to discipline procedures agreed upon.

Partnership between parents, teachers, students, and administration is paramount to educational success.

The best schools value a healthy partnership between parents, teachers, students, and administration based on mutual respect, shared goals, and accountability. (If you're a homeschooler, that means you look for co-ops that use these same principles—teaching subjects that aren't your forte and addressing these same concepts.) There is always open communication between all parties. Your child's teacher sends emails regarding assignments, happenings in class, etc. You receive mailings and emails from administration about changes in policy or events at school. You have the ability to track easily how your child is doing in class and have access to communicate directly with the teacher.

Parents and grandparents are encouraged to volunteer on campus and welcomed in the classroom for various activities.

The school board is unified in making good decisions on behalf of the students. Many times boards are at odds with three-to-two splits on votes and stay that way in true "us/them" fashion. Boards that are always split don't bode well for faculty, staff, or curriculum longevity, the school's budget, or the continuity and quality of education.

Will every school you check out have all these traits—even those considered the "best schools"? No, because every school is unique. You need to decide which of these traits are nonnegotiables for you and your family as you search for the right schooling option for your child.

My Bias: A Classical Model School

I'll freely admit it. My favorite kind of school is one that follows a "classical" model. Classical education is an integrated approach based on the traditions of Western culture, as understood and taught in classical antiquity and the Middle Ages, that emphasizes virtues (truth, goodness, honesty, beauty), the study of Latin, learning by the trivium (grammar, logic, rhetoric), and developing critical thinking.

My daughter Krissy taught in a classical school. Two of my grandkids went through that school. I saw the wonderful, practical, and imaginative results of children who learned to work independently and also creatively in groups. They were challenged by what they learned and motivated because learning was fun. That's why I founded Leman Academy of Excellence as a classical charter school.

What do I love about classical schools? They *invite* children into the learning process. They don't drag them in, kicking and screaming. Classical schools take advantage of children's natural curiosity to propel their education. Such a school model also aligns with my basic belief that a school should deal with the whole child, not just a portion. I strongly believe that in today's global but relationally fragmented world, faculty and staff should be as concerned with teaching good manners and courtesy as they are with teaching math and science. The classical model is steeped in virtues.

A classical school also helps to prepare kids for real life outside of school by hands-on learning and partners closely with the parent in the home. At Leman Academy of Excellence, we place an emphasis on families spending time together. For example, our policy is never to give a test on a Monday after vacation. Vacations and holidays should be family time, not study time for students.

Our emphasis on families is also why our faculty and staff work hard to get to know students and their families. Last August, in the Arizona heat of 100 degrees, two top administrators were out at the curb, bringing young kids safely from their cars into the school building. At the end of the day, they were out there again, taking the kids back to their cars and engaging with the parents.

Little things like that reveal the heart of a school—what its values truly are. They also pave the way for a close educational partnership with the parents. Let's say Michael has a bad day at school. He has a hard time listening and doing his work. After his teacher walks with him out to the car, she says to his parent, "Michael has something to discuss with you today about his behavior in the classroom and his lack of work. And he has a note for you as well."

With a kind, firm statement, the teacher serves the tennis ball of responsibility into Michael's court. There's no wiggle room.

Mom knows things are not well.

Michael is put on the spot. He's the one who will have to fork over the teacher's handwritten note about his behavior that day.

I guarantee that as soon as that car door closes, Michael's mom—if she's like 99 percent of moms on the planet—will turn toward him with eagle eyes. "Michael! What on earth did you do in school today?"

But it's even better if she says nothing and lets him stew in his own juices just a bit. Sometimes a little fear of consequences can go a long way toward prompting change.

So the smart parent waits—not only for her kid's welfare but also because she can choose how to respond rather than react emotionally to the surprise of the event. The latter will make a much greater impact for a teachable moment Michael will remember for a long time.

When issues are handled so that the child has to pony up to what he did and be held responsible, and the parent has time to think through her strategy, chances are good that the child won't try that behavior again anytime soon and his work ethic will greatly improve.

> The classical model uses the historical timeline to teach sequentially, integrating all subjects.

The classical model also values languages and the development of language and logic. At Leman Academy, we teach children Spanish in kindergarten, Latin in third grade, and logic in sixth grade.

The classical model uses the historical timeline to teach sequentially, integrating all subjects. For example, if your class is studying the World War II time period, they study Germany in geography, Hitler in history, *The Diary of Anne Frank* in reading, and famous German composers and artists from that era in music and art classes. It's a fabulous way to teach and a fun way for children to learn, absorb, and understand entire chunks of history.

At Leman Academy, we also mix and match with children working independently and as group members on projects.

Last year, kids in one of the sixth-grade classes created their own newspaper. As soon as I stepped on campus one afternoon, the child who wrote the cover feature ran up to me.

"Dr. Leman, Dr. Leman, you have to read this!" he exclaimed.

He was so excited he nearly shoved his article in my face. He was proud of his creation and wanted to make sure I read it. I chuckled, wondering if a future journalist was in the room. I wouldn't be surprised.

The feature of the paper was all about Genghis Khan. All the kids became instant reporters and got their feet wet in figuring out how to put together a newspaper. One of the children decided to "interview" Genghis Khan's grandfather and asked questions such as, "What kind of a little kid was Genghis as he was growing up?"

The result was creativity at its finest. Not only did children learn about a different time period—from the 1100s to the 1200s—and the terrifying warrior king of the Mongol Empire, but they simultaneously experienced what it was like to have the career of a newspaper reporter. When those kids are 40, they'll still know who Genghis Khan is and remember creating that newspaper. And because they are learning how to integrate different subjects, they'll develop critical thinking that will follow them and serve them well all their lives.

That's even more reason for me to love the classical model.

Contrast that to what many schools focus on. As I've walked into numerous elementary schools through the years, I've seen a common trait. Nearly every classroom has been loaded with worksheets—reams of them. The kind where, even if you know how to do one math problem, you have to do five sheets' worth of them. I couldn't run quickly enough from those places. In my biased view, loading kids with boring worksheets is not an education. It's rote learning that just kills time when it could be far better spent.

In a classical school, a rich conversation develops in the classroom, where the teacher engages with the students to pull out things they already know but haven't yet processed. For example, a first-grade teacher holds up a painting of a farmscape to the class. "Class, what do you think?" she asks. There's no lecture about farms, no preamble telling the kids what they should think as they stare at the picture.

Kid 1: "It's a farm."

Teacher: "Why do you suppose the artist painted this farm-scape?"

Kid 2: "Maybe he grew up on a farm."

Teacher: "Well, what do you find on a farm?"

Arms are flung in the air as answers explode like popcorn in a kettle. "Horses. Chickens. Hay. Manure!"

Kid 4 puts his hand up. "My grandpa has a farm. It has wheat, corn, and barley."

Teacher: "Ah, interesting. Do any of you know what wheat looks like? What corn looks like? What about barley?"

The teacher effectively draws the kids into the conversation. The room rings with lively questions and answers, and these continue as information is shared around the dinner table after the children arrive home.

We don't often give kids enough credit for knowing or contributing what they know. Instead, we spend our time *lecturing* them rather than *engaging* with them. When they can contribute to learning, the process is enormously more fun, and education sticks.

I strongly believe that education is important, but it's not the most important thing in life. Somebody will always be smarter and better than your child. However, if you teach them to have a kind heart toward others, they like who they are, they know their gifts, and their self-worth isn't tied to their performance, they'll already be ahead of the pack in life.

School doesn't make your child somebody. They already are somebody. But education furthers their knowledge, gives them a new window to the world, and puts the finest sheen on their natural skills.

9

Your Personal Menu to Educational Success

Taking what you've learned and turning it into a practical plan.

You've learned in this book about schooling options, your child's strengths and weaknesses, and how your expectations and background influence your view of educational success. We've also identified some key traits of the best schools. Now it's your turn to take all the a la carte items and assemble them into a personalized menu for your child's educational success. You might want to use a notebook to scribble your thoughts as you proceed through this chapter.

And don't worry. You don't have to complete this chapter in one sitting. Take all the time you need. Just do one section at a time when you have a quiet moment.

Your Child

1. Learning styles

Recognizing the ways your child learns will greatly help you in identifying the best learning environment for his particular needs.

- Visual/spatial: Your child learns through what he sees, such as images and pictures.
- Auditory/musical: Your child learns through sound, such as music and hearing a concept explained.
- Verbal/linguistic: Your child learns through words, both in writing and in speech.
- Kinesthetic/physical: Your child learns through physical motion and the sense of touch.
- Logical/mathematical: Your child learns through logic and reasoning.
- Social/interpersonal: Your child learns by working in groups and with other people.
- Solitary/intrapersonal: Your child learns by working alone.

2. Natural bents

- What natural talents does your child have?
- If he's young, what toys does he play with most? Blocks? Crayons and paper? Puzzles?

- If she's older, what interests does she gravitate toward? Sports? Music? Problem solving? Technology? Working with her hands?

3. Personality and working styles

Consider the following for your child:

- Activity level: Is he constantly on the move? Or can he play alone and quietly by himself?
- Attention span: Is it long, short, or based on the task?
- Work style: Does she prefer to be alone or with others in groups?
- Social interaction: Does he crave it for motivation? Or does he need quiet?
- Risk-taking level: Is she cautious about anything new? Or does she plunge right in?
- Challenge level: Is he driven by challenges, seeing them as hurdles to overcome? Or does he feel incapacitated by hurdles or find them overwhelming?
- Finishing level: Does she finish what she starts? Or does she start multiple projects and not finish them?
- Curiosity level: Does he ask frequently how something works? Or does he tend to simply accept that something works?

4. Birth order

How do the following characteristics influence your thinking about your child's schooling options?

- Firstborn: well organized, serious, scholarly, perfectionistic, natural leader, reliable, conscientious, likes a road map and not curveballs, highly motivated

- Only child: high achiever, black-and-white thinker, little adult, believes failure isn't an option, has high expectations, deliberate, cautious

- Middleborn: avoids conflict, mediator, compromising, goes in the opposite direction of the firstborn, loyal to friends, secretive and good at keeping secrets, needs peer network

- Lastborn: charming, fun loving, manipulative, loves attention, treats life as a party, affectionate, doesn't always take work seriously

If you have more than one child, would you consider sending them to different schools? Why or why not?

5. Future plans

What do you want your child to be like 10 to 20 years down the road? Which of the following are most important to you?

- To be able to think for herself
- To make good decisions

- To be a person of integrity who does what he says he will
- To be honest and trustworthy
- To care about others
- To work hard and to be able to accomplish her goals
- To not give up, even when times are hard
- To use his skills to better humankind.
- How do you expect a school to partner with you—if at all—in the development of these skills?

=*You*=

1. Which of these is most important to you?

- High academics for college readiness
- A match for your child's developing talents
- Curriculum that mirrors and enhances your belief system
- Peers similar to your child in background and socio-economic level
- The opportunity to interact with children of diverse backgrounds
- The cost of the school (free vs. tuition based)
- Involvement in and/or control over your child's educational path
- The ability to understand and compete in a global economy

2. Parenting style

Which seems most like you? How do you think that style influences your schooling choices?

- Authoritarian: You tend to micromanage your child, lay down the law, make decisions for her, and keep an eye on her schedule.
- Permissive: You tend to rescue your child from consequences, always defend and back him even when

he's wrong, do his homework, make life easy for him, problem solve for him, and overindulge him.

- Authoritative: You let reality be the teacher so your child experiences the consequences of her actions. You have high expectations, provide age-appropriate choices, and allow your child to make her own decisions.

3. Personality type

Which seems most like you? How does your personality impact your schooling choices?

- Controller: You like to be in charge, have high expectations, crave order, and don't do well in chaos.

- Pleaser: You go out of your way to make others happy (often by sacrificing your own desires), sometimes take the blame for what isn't your fault, and rarely stand up for yourself.

- Charmer: You like being the center of attention, pout if you don't get your way, and are used to getting what you want.

- Victim: You resent the educational advantages others have, feel like you're always blamed when things go wrong, and believe that you're unlucky and that life has given you a raw deal.

········ **4. Birth order** ···

How does your birth order influence your view of academic life and the schooling options you might pursue?

- Firstborn: You expect a lot out of your child. Seeing As on your child's report card is extremely important and nonnegotiable. Academic progress is much more important to you than social interaction.

- Only child: You've always worked independently, so you don't expect to have to check on your child's academic progress to keep him motivated. You also don't understand why siblings would compete with each other, or why they would need to go to different schools. *Just pick the best school*, you think, *and send all the kids there. Streamlined. Easy. And they all get a top-notch education.*

- Middleborn: Your child attending a school where she can interact easily with peers and develop a solid network of friends is very important—likely more important than the academic environment.

- Lastborn: The social environment of a school is important to you. So are additional activities in which your child can get involved for a broader school experience.

········ **5. Expectations for your child** ·······································

- Are they reasonable based on your child's natural talents?

- Are they colored by your own unfulfilled desires?
- Are they flexible or inflexible?
- Are they based on your real child or the ideal child you're projecting?

=*The School*=

- Charter school: A free, independently run public school of choice that has specific missions, programs, performance goals, and methods to assess academic performance. Based on the three-stage approach to education—grammar, logic, and rhetoric.

- Home school: Education of children at home by their parents or a chosen tutor.

- Magnet school: An upper-end public school that offers programs and instruction designed to attract a diverse body of competent, focused, serious students.

- Military school: A targeted educational institution that prepares young men and women for service in the US military—Army, Navy, Air Force, Coast Guard, or Marine Corps. Usually also a boarding school.

- Private school (religious, parochial, or other): A tuition-based school supported by a private organization or a group of private individuals rather than by local, state, or national fees, as public or charter schools are. Can be religiously affiliated or a denominational school. Can teach faith-based education along with regular academic subjects, with the goal of impressing specific religious beliefs on the students. Or can teach denominational beliefs but also cover academic subjects from all angles,

201

maintaining a fine distinction between academics and religion.

- Public school: A tuition-free school operated by the local, state, and national governments. Includes primary and secondary schools.

- Virtual/online school: Provides internet resources—lessons, teaching, and homework—for multiple schooling options but operates primarily through online methods. Can be a public, private, or home school.

- Vocational school: Provides high school students with practical education and job training for specific jobs and careers. Typically offers focused programs that swiftly pave the way to the workforce after graduation rather than focusing on academic training for scholars pursuing professional careers, but can also include academics. Usually government owned or at least government supported. Typically extend for two years rather than four years.

2. What type of school best matches your child in the following?

- Structure
- Philosophy
- Learning style
- Atmosphere and environment
- Focus and gifts

- Extracurricular options (sports, music, art, other programs)

3. What type of school best matches your goals in the following?

- Safety
  - doctor or nurse on campus
  - how medicine and allergies are handled
  - procedures in place
  - metal detectors
  - bulletproof doors
  - drills conducted with local law enforcement and fire departments
- Nature and range of curriculum
  - pre-K available (half day or full day?)
  - kindergarten available (half day or full day?)
  - grades 1–12 available
  - Common Core
  - classical or other model
  - basic curriculum (math, science, history, English) and intensity of curriculum
  - PE (regular, specialized)
  - art (types of classes)
  - music (classroom, band, orchestra)
  - foreign language (which ones, and for how many years?)
- Enrollment procedures
  - waiting list (how long, possibility of getting in)

- testing required for admittance (which test, how and when it's given—such as DIBELS, or Dynamic Indicators of Basic Early Literary Skills—to establish baseline of comprehension)
- steps to enroll your child
- fees, if any (returnable or not)

- Transportation and proximity to your home
  - buses
  - carpools
  - cost, if any

- Belief system
  - aligns with your faith
  - teaches only agreed-upon beliefs
  - provides broad views of social, scientific, and cultural issues

- Family values
  - policy regarding leave for family trips, death in family, etc.
  - homework on weekends and church nights

- Faculty and staff
  - certified and qualified in field
  - expectations of students
  - style of interaction
  - engagement level with the students
  - how they communicate (email, phone, conferences)
  - view of partnership with parents
  - available for extra tutoring (or can refer students to specialized tutor)
  - available for music lessons on-site

- School policies
  - class size
  - availability of aides
  - how volunteers are used
  - dress code
  - discipline (bullying, tardiness, detention)
  - excused and unexcused absences
  - missed homework
  - cell phone usage
- Fees
  - tuition
  - books
  - field trips
  - lunch program, if any
  - fund-raising activities (and required or not?)
  - after-school clubs (sports, drama, music)
  - scholarships available (if any)

4. What additional needs do you have that you'd like a school to meet?

- Programs for special education (autism, visual impairments, speech pathology, reading comprehension, physical challenges, mental and emotional challenges, Down syndrome)
  - part of the regular classroom or a separate classroom
  - assistance by aides

- same or different standards for learning and testing
- work with IEPs and 504 Plans
- ESL (English as a Second Language) student
  - tutoring
  - aides available
- Gifted programs
  - changes in curriculum, if any
- Counselor on-site
  - vocational or occupational counseling
  - mental challenges
- Before- or after-school care
  - pick-up and drop-off procedure
  - earliest time to drop off
  - latest time to pick up
- Add your own points that haven't been covered

Mixing and Matching Your Own Schooling Menu

Now, parent, it's time to use your expertise. Start with the facts you've gathered in this chapter about you, your child, and the schools you've identified as potential options. Which schooling options are rising to the front of your mind now? They might be ones you never would have thought of previously, but they seem to perfectly suit the three most important basics of education:

- academic excellence
- real-life application
- a perfect match for your child's uniqueness

A quality education is a wonderful thing. It grooms students to become contributing members of society. It helps them develop critical thinking so they can compete well in our increasingly global world. It poises them to become future leaders in their family, in their community, nationally, and internationally.

Now is your time to step up as your child's educational advocate. After all, no one knows your child better than you. On top of that, you've learned a few things yourself along the way, and you're smarter than you were when you first held that child in your arms.

You now know that you don't need to have all of life's answers tucked in your back pocket for you to move ahead. After you weigh the options, you don't have to worry about making the wrong choice. You can confidently make the best choice—for now. If the option needs to change later, so be it. You can wisely meet that challenge if and when it comes your way.

I've said it before, and I'll say it again for emphasis. What you teach your child at home is the most important schooling she'll ever have. That's because you really are the main entrée in your child's education—and in her heart. Everything else is an a la carte option.

ASK DR. LEMAN

The hottest questions parents ask about education and my time-tested answers.

Attitudes and Motivation

Q: My day always gets off to a rough start, because my daughter is negative about everything. She doesn't get up when I ask her to, she doesn't want the breakfast I've prepared, and she always whines, "Why do I have to go to school today?" I hate it when she asks questions she already knows the answers to. It drives me up the wall.

Within a few minutes of her attitude, *I* have an attitude that I can't shake off. When I finally get her out the door—usually just in time to run for the bus—I've screamed so much at her (and yes, I admit, even called her names) that I spend the rest of the day feeling guilty about it. How can I turn this craziness around?

A: You're trying to do too much for your daughter in the morning. There's a schedule in your mind for what the morning should look like, and you try to move things along quickly. Your daughter senses that and digs in (my guess is that you're both controller personalities, so you butt heads easily). She refuses that breakfast and asks all those stupid questions just to engage you in battle. She really doesn't want an answer about why she has to go to school. She just wants to fight with you.

But here's a secret. Fighting is always an act of cooperation. When a kid verbally paws at you, she's saying, "Okay, let's see how much I can ramp up this battle." She wants you to continue wallowing in negativity, because that gives her the adrenaline rush of maintaining control over your household.

So here's my advice. Go ahead and make her breakfast. When she says, "I don't like that, and I'm not going to eat it," don't say a word. Just turn your back and walk out of the breakfast area.

"Wait a minute," you might be saying. "What does that accomplish? My kid will be hungry until lunch if she doesn't eat breakfast."

Well, is that your problem? A few hunger pangs won't kill her, but they might serve as a wake-up call. Hunger is a great motivator. If she misses breakfast a few times because of her attitude, the reality is that she'll change her tune when her stomach growls at school.

Even better, you didn't give her the chance to say she didn't want to go to school, because you exited the room. You're also conveniently not available until after the bus has already left.

I can guarantee your daughter will be sitting on that bus with a puzzled expression.

When she comes in the door from school that afternoon, she'll try to continue her usual dog-and-pony show. "What was with you this morning, Mom? What's your problem?"

You give her a cool stare. "I don't appreciate your attitude. I am willing to make breakfast for you and help you get out the door. But every morning you basically beat me up with your words, telling me I'm not a good mother because you don't like your breakfast. All you want to do is fight with me. Well, I'm not playing that game any longer. I'm out. If you want to continue to play, that's up to you, but you'll be by yourself. I'll leave breakfast for you on the counter, and it's your choice to eat it or not. But I won't be available."

Again, you go into a different room in the house, leaving an openmouthed daughter in the kitchen.

Sure, your daughter will test you the next morning, but you do what you say. You make her breakfast, leave it on the counter, then make yourself unavailable. Your daughter doesn't have to be a rocket scientist to get the picture that things have changed around your house.

All you have to do is stick to the plan, Mom. I know you can do it.

Q: Now that my son has entered high school, he's stopped talking to me. All I get is a grunt or a turned head after school. This is the kid who always used to snuggle up next to me and wanted me to read to him and ruffle his hair. I keep wondering, *Is it the school or what? Is he under too much pressure because I did the wrong thing putting him in a private school that's known for its hard academics?*

A: The best thing you can do is develop what I call a "third ear" and "third eye"—the kind of hearing and seeing that goes beyond the norm. This is important when you have adolescents and teenagers. They're in a tumultuous time, pressured by a lot of changeable winds at school. Academics are tougher. Kids have more activities on their platter. Sometimes they just get overwhelmed.

Your "third ear" allows you to hear what your kid is saying through his grunt. That simple sound is actually filled with this weighty monologue: "Mom, I've had a really long day today, and I'm just not up for conversation right now. I need to be left alone because I've got a headache from all the chaos today, and I'm trying to process my thoughts."

Your "third eye" detects the tiredness in his eyes and the dejected slump in his posture as he turns away from you toward the car door.

All that body language should tell you clearly that now isn't the time to have a conversation. Give your son time to eat (even if it's four bowls of cereal, food does wonders to perk up a dragging teenager) and then detox by himself in his room. Eventually he'll come out of his teenage cave, and when he does, he doesn't need questions fired at him. Just a simple, "Wow, you seem a little down today. If you ever want to talk about it, I'm all ears" will do the trick.

He might not respond right away. You might even wonder if he heard you. But rest assured—he did.

It might be later that night or even several days before he talks. But if you've had a good relationship with him over the years, he will talk sometime. When he does, shut your mouth. Focus on listening. Watch his expressions, feel his heart. By communicating with you, he's saying, "Mom, I

212

trust you with my feelings enough that I'm daring to talk with you about what happened."

Maybe he got shot down for trying to help somebody at school. Or he was betrayed by a friend. Or he didn't make the team.

Don't ask questions. If you pry or interrogate him, he'll shut you out of his life.

Instead, use leading statements such as, "No wonder you had a rough day. That would have bothered me too," or, "Tell me more about that."

When you say things like that, you're telling your son, "You're important to me. What you think, experience, and feel are important to me too. I'm in your court. I always will be."

In the interim, while he's in that teenage cave, keep your mouth shut, especially when you want his to open. Yes, it's hard, but you're the adult, and you can do this.

Curriculum, Homework, and Skills

Q: Studying and grades are just not important to my son, Dan. How can I get him to take them more seriously?

A: Let's give your question a little more context. Take a look at your life first—all the things you do routinely that take up your week. It might be your job, your spouse or significant other, acting as taxi driver for your kids, housework, cooking, and/or cleaning. In other words, you do your part to make your home and family run effectively.

I heartily believe that every person has to be a participating member of their family if they want to enjoy the inherent benefits of living in that family. Dan has a job too—going to school. If he isn't fulfilling it by taking studying and his grades seriously, he isn't doing that job well.

Dan needs a good dose of Vitamin N—No. If you know he has a test coming up in history and he hasn't cracked open his history book all week, it's time for you to play a little parental poker with that kid and use one of the aces up your sleeve.

Right after dinner, he announces, "Dad, I need you to take me to Adam's. You can pick me up at nine."

You lift an eyebrow. "You're not going anywhere. I know you haven't studied for your history test, and it's tomorrow."

"But I have to go. We talked about it this afternoon. We're all getting together at Adam's to play Call of Duty 5. I'll study for the test when I get back," he says and throws on his jacket.

Now, you could spout more than a few words, including, "Listen up, bubba. I've got news for you. I'm the parent here." But you don't, because as much as you want to throw such retorts into his self-satisfied face, you know that will only breed rebellion. Instead, you play your ace dad card.

"That's a no-go, Dan," you say firmly. "Your history comes first. You know studying is a top priority in this house. Everybody in this family works. I work downtown, and I take my job seriously. I can't leave until it's done for the day. Your work right now is being a student. You might want to think about taking it more seriously."

Then you turn your back and walk away. You didn't tell him he was a bad kid or that you'd take him to Adam's when he finished studying. No, the conversation is over for the evening, and you left the responsibility for his lack of studying right where it should be—with your son.

He'll likely try to follow you and argue, but don't engage. Your son has to find an unembarrassing way (good luck with that!) to back out of the deal. Sure, he'll paint you as the bad guy to his friends. He'll probably kick his history book around his bedroom.

But eventually he might open that book. Studying may suddenly have become a bit more important to him.

Q: Jasmine is in fifth grade, and she always has tons of homework to do at night. I never had homework as a kid until I went to high school. Is she not getting enough done at school? Or is there more homework these days? What do you think is a reasonable amount of work for a child that age to do at night?

A: Every school has different expectations of homework, so it would be good to ask her teachers that question. Many charter schools have higher expectations for homework than public schools do. Private schools often will have more than vocational schools. At least that's what people tend to think.

But to me, not all homework is created equal. There is quality homework, which helps a child learn a subject and develop her thinking powers. Then there's busywork. As I tell parents who are visiting potential schools, "If you see lots of worksheets in the classroom, run and don't stop until you're out the door." Worksheets are a symptom of bad teaching. They fill time but don't extend learning. When a child learns how to do a math problem, she can do three to five similar problems to solidify the concept. She doesn't need to have five full worksheets of them that week.

In a similar way, simply opening a book, going to page 34, and answering questions 4, 5, and 6 doesn't do much to educate children either (other than teach them how to flip pages as quickly as possible).

I believe that the majority of schoolwork should be done in the classroom. You have a workday, and school is your child's workday. When kids are home, the majority of that time should be for personal and family time. On occasion there might be extra work—a book report or a science project. But in general, their workday should be over.

The goal of education is to create critical thinkers who have a broad knowledge about the world, not to encourage hamsters to run endlessly and pointlessly on a wheel.

Q: Melanie, our only child, is really shy. She tends to hang back in crowds and hides behind me if there's someone she doesn't know. She's 4½, and my husband is pushing me to get her into preschool. He thinks she needs to have more social interaction with other kids. But I don't know if she's ready for preschool. Your advice?

A: One of the many reasons to send children to preschool is to allow them to interact more socially with others outside their family. The same is true for kindergarten. Without rubbing shoulders with peers she doesn't know, little Melanie can easily come to believe that she's the center of the universe. But what she wants isn't always what she gets. She has to learn to share and cooperate with others.

If she's an only child, social interaction with peers is even more important. She doesn't have siblings to compete with her, so she's been fully in the spotlight of your attention.

Because she's been surrounded by adults, she's much more comfortable with them than with kids her own age. She likes things to be predictable and controlled. But children who are 4 and 5 are certainly not always in the "predictable" category.

There's something else you may not realize about your little angel. All social behavior serves a purpose in a child's life. Consider this idea: if Melanie acts shy and hides behind you, you pave the way for her in meeting new people.

Melanie may act shy, but she's actually a very powerful child. Even though she's only the size of a yardstick, she's already making adults much bigger than her approach her in a very definite, precise way. Because her behavior is working, that "win" increases the probability of her becoming even more powerful.

"That can't be right," you might say. "Some people are just shy. I was legitimately shy as a child. I wasn't a powerful kid."

Well, you can believe what you want to believe. But based on my 40-plus years of working with people psychologically, I don't believe that for a minute. Powerful kids can be loud or speak in whispers. They can be aggressive in their behavior or quietly manipulative.

Tell me if I'm wrong, but you and your husband probably walk on eggshells around Melanie. You don't want to disturb your little cherub's psyche, after all. But she's in charge of the show, and she's getting a good one—for free. Adults make fools of themselves in front of shy children as they try to coax them out from behind Mama's legs to say "hello" or "thank you."

Guess who has full control of that social situation? Little Melanie.

What do you usually say when she refuses to talk or greet someone? "Well, I guess Melanie's not talking today." Then you go back to your conversation.

Problem is, if your child is a powerful one, you'll feel a little tug on your jeans in a short while. That's all calculated precisely, Mom. Melanie is at work to keep you needlessly engaged in a tug-of-war for your attention. She doesn't like it that you're paying attention to someone else, since in her mind she's the center of the universe.

She also might talk so softly that you can't hear her. You know what she's likely asking for, but to hear the question you have to lean way over, next to her ear.

Guess who's controlling that situation too?

But what would happen if you removed the tugging hand from your jeans and then ignored her? Would she melt down or get more frantic in her tugging?

Or what if you said to her, "Honey, I can't hear you" when she spoke too softly, and then you walked to another room to take care of your next task? Would your little muffin scramble after you and try to get your attention again?

Both responses mean you have a very powerful child who has learned how to work you to her best advantage.

Again, there is a purpose to every social behavior your child exhibits. The technical term for it is *purposive behavior*. You don't hear that term every day, but it's an important one to know.

In a preschool situation, your child will continue that purposive behavior as long as it works to her advantage. If she's shy, she can stand in the corner and wait until an aide comes to get her and draw her into the group. And others might help her more with her work.

218

My advice is, the sooner you can get that child into pre-school, the better. Letting your teacher know up front about the secret you've discovered would also be a good thing. Handling her powerful behavior now makes a lot more sense than trying to manage it when she's 16 and behind the wheel of a car, don't you think?

(For a preschool readiness checklist, see chapter 6.)

Q: As I've checked out schools, I've noticed that a lot of them now teach Spanish, and sometimes French or Latin. How important do you think learning a second language is? Spanish I can see, since some people I know speak it. But French or Latin? When would my son ever use those? Cade is just an average student. I think he's going to end up working somehow with his hands—maybe some kind of a trade.

A: Schools today are starting to teach second languages as early as kindergarten because such an education model matches how children absorb information. Young children are very receptive to learning dual languages. In fact, 18-month-olds are wired to be able to receive a language.

Children who do well in language generally do well in math. Learning a new language, even one like French or Latin that may truly seem "foreign" to you, builds psychological muscles that will serve your child well in life. Also, since so many English words have Latin derivatives, learning Latin expands your child's ability to understand his primary language. So why not learn multiple languages at the same time?

I know a family in which the dad is Chinese, the mom is Korean, and both work at American companies. The couple's only shared language is English. Their 2-year-old daughter

219

is learning English, Chinese, and Korean simultaneously. (Wow, talk about an intriguing trilingual résumé that kid will have someday. She'll be an international relations, FBI, or CIA dream catch.)

Think about today's global economy. It's a whole new world, even from the one you grew up in not so long ago. People who can speak, read, and write in two or more languages at an early age will have a total advantage over others in our rapidly expanding world.

Where I live in Tucson, Arizona, there is a high percentage of Latinos. Spanish speakers are prevalent here. Those who are proficient in both Spanish and English are easy and necessary hires for nearly every type of business.

Let's say your son does end up working in a machine shop. Well, he won't be working solo, and Spanish is one of the major languages in the world, with a growing population. He's likely to have Spanish-speaking co-workers. If so, who do you think could rise to a management position?

That's right. Your son.

The best time for children to learn languages is when they're young. It gets tougher for brain waves to repattern themselves to learn a new language once you're a grandpa, like me.

If your child masters a foreign language, the world will open up to him and be his oyster, as the old expression says. Most colleges today require at least two years of foreign language for you to even get in the door. More prestigious universities require three years.

That's why, at Leman Academy of Excellence, we take advantage of the tremendous ability of children to learn languages.

Not to mention Cade will look pretty cool when he travels to Mexico and South America and can order dinner in *español*.

Q: My dad always drummed into us kids the importance of getting the four basics down—math, science, history, and English. We grew up in a farming community and didn't have much free time. School even shut down when it was harvesttime, because kids needed to help their parents.

I remember wishing when I was in fourth grade that I could take an art class, play an instrument, or be part of a sports team. But I didn't have the opportunity to do any of that.

Now that I have a child who's going into school and I'm living in a different town, I think a lot about that. I hope Emma has the chance to do things she'd like to do. But many of the schools I've checked into for her seem to have cut what they call "the extras." So am I wrong? How important are "the extras" in education?

A: You tell me. You're still thinking about "the extras" a couple decades later, so they're not extras to you. Clearly they're important to you personally, and you want Emma to have a shot at what you missed out on.

My personal view is that athletics, art, and music are very important in the development of the whole child in education. What would our world be like without those things? No Chicago Cubs winning the World Series for the first time in 108 years? No Picasso paintings? No Beethoven's Fifth Symphony?

That's why I love and highly believe in the classical model and established a school with that model. We offer music, art, and PE as a central part of our curriculum. They aren't add-ons. They're part of the centerpiece of learning, just like math, science, history, and English. We also have after-school sports clubs.

I do realize why schools are cutting athletics, music, and art. Many schools who are faced with budget cuts and teacher cuts have to make some tough choices. To them, core curriculum is far more important. Anything else is an extra and often has to go.

If you want your child to have a well-rounded education, go after schools that include athletics, art, and music as part of their standard curriculum. You'll be glad you did. So will Emma.

Q: My children have been attending a public school, but this coming year we're switching to a private school. I know my two older kids will adjust fine, but I'm a little worried about my third grader, Stevie. He struggles with math as it is, and the new school says they have high expectations for academics. Fourth-grade math there is like fifth-grade math in the public school. If Stevie had a hard time even with third-grade math in the public school (which some people say is dumbed down), will he be able to keep up? What do you think?

A: The first six weeks in any school system is usually a repeat of what kids learned in the last semester of the previous year. Some children tend to struggle at first, especially if they didn't grasp the concepts the previous year. However, most private schools won't take a child they don't think can succeed in their school. So it's likely Stevie can catch on and do well.

Also, maybe a more rigorous curriculum will be just what the doctor ordered to motivate your child. Isn't it better for him to be challenged and work hard than to coast along and do the bare minimum? Yes, he'll have to make an extra effort, but there's nothing wrong with a little academic sweat now and then.

Kids usually live up to the expectations you put on them—whether you're the parent or the teacher. Take it from someone who knows. I was a troublemaker all throughout school and regularly ran over teachers who were weak. I rarely paid attention in any class. However, there were two straight-talking teachers I never challenged—ever. They were known for doing what they said they'd do. I always paid attention in those classes, and wonder of wonders, I even learned something.

You might be surprised what a little challenge will accomplish in your youngest child's life.

Q: The school my daughter attends does a lot with memorization and giving speeches. She hates both of those. How important are they really as a part of education? And if they are important, how do I convey that to her?

A: Here's a question for you. What is the one thing that adults in general fear most?

Speaking in public!

That's why memorization and giving speeches are critical skills to develop in school. If children learn how to handle both skills capably from the beginning, they won't be tongue-tied and nerve-racked when they have to do them later. Talk about great training for life. You won't interview well for a job without those skills. You won't get your point across in an executive meeting without them. You won't make a sale to a potential customer without them. People who can speak well publicly come out winners in life because they learn how to dominate a room.

Children also gain confidence from memorizing and being able to repeat something verbally in front of a group. That's why kindergarteners at the Leman Academy of Excellence recite verbatim a long poem or narrative. They are capable of memorizing several paragraph chunks, then get up in front of the class and recite individually and as part of a group.

Is it easy for every child? No, some really struggle with memorizing and public speaking for a while. But struggling is a normal part of education. It's okay and expected. Eventually, most children will master memorization and public speaking and do a beautiful job.

I'm constantly amazed at what young kids can do. I now know that first graders can conjugate verbs and diagram sentences. They even know what the object of a preposition is. We adults don't give them enough credit.

When children are able to articulate ideas and thoughts, they gain confidence to face the world in general.

Q: How do I know if my child is ready for kindergarten? He turns 5 in August, the week before the local kindergarten starts. Maybe it's just because I'm a protective mom who can't let go of her first kid (I have three, and he's the oldest), but I really want Grant's first experience with school to be positive. If the stress is too much or he misses me too much, he won't enjoy the experience or thrive there. What do you think?

A: Good for you for wanting his first experience with school to be positive! You're already on the right track. Many parents push their kids too early into kindergarten, but you seem to have a very balanced view.

Today's kindergarten is very different from what it was when you were growing up. It's like your first grade was. It's academically based. Many kids are already reading in kindergarten, and they're quick to absorb new concepts. The days of focusing on Play-Doh and crayons are over. Your child may be able to count to 10 or, if pressed, to 20. But does Grant know his colors and recognize the letters of the alphabet? Can he write his name and follow simple instructions? These are all clues for kindergarten readiness for a 5-year-old.

Also, is Grant socially ready for kindergarten? Is he capable of sharing? How he does with his younger siblings is a good clue as to how he'll interact in kindergarten with his peers once he's comfortable with them.

Children are not natural sharers. Two- and three-year-olds are famous for their "mine, mine" statements. That's a specific developmental stage. But to become ready for school and social interaction outside the home, children need to develop some "others" focus.

Kindergarten is a big deal. You're right not to rush into it but to carefully think it through.

The first proving ground in life is school, so you do want Grant to have a positive experience. If he truly is ready, he'll be put in a position where he has a great shot at being successful. If in doubt, especially for boys, give them that extra year.

Q: Kindergarten seems to be so different from what I thought it would be. What's a typical kindergarten morning like at Leman Academy?

A: Step into the room with me for a quick view.

Kids start the day by hanging up their backpacks, then moving toward their tables. First, the teacher gets the kids' attention by saying a simple phrase that's unique to him or her. The phrase is the same every day, so kids learn it as part of the routine. They know it means they need to get in their seats and pay attention. And all it takes is a few words from a master teacher.

Next is the Pledge of Allegiance. One child gets picked to be the leader. He stands in front of the group, places his hand over his heart, and leads the class in the pledge.

Those who don't know child psychology might take a look and think, *What's going on here? Are they trying to make clones of the kids?*

No, this is part of the training for what happens every day in kindergarten. Kids who are 5 and 6 love and thrive on routine. It lends stability and safety to the classroom. It also helps to draw children of diverse backgrounds into a cohesive group.

The first few days of kindergarten resemble individual sheep scattered around a mountainside. They aren't sure of their direction. But with a few deft moves by the mama sheep, who has been around the mountain for a while and can judge the personalities of her newest lambs, those sheep soon begin to feel and move like a single flock.

Q: I want my child to have the option to get into the best colleges and universities, if that's what he decides. What educational steps do I need to take along the way to accomplish that? Luke is entering high school this coming year.

A: Quality high schools pay attention to and usually keep records of the colleges and universities their graduates are accepted into. Why? Because it's a great advertisement for the school. If their graduates are accepted into top-notch universities, it's a big compliment to the academic excellence of the high school.

Recently a Catholic school in Arizona took out a full-page ad in their local paper, listing the universities and colleges their graduates would attend in the fall. The prestigious list included Harvard, Yale, and Northwestern. You can bet that every parent who has their eye on the prize of the best universities in America will take a careful look at enrolling their child in that high school.

Other steps you can take are making sure that Luke has four years of math, science, history, and English—even if four years of each are not required at his high school. He should also take at least three years of the same foreign language. Extracurricular involvements that show a dedication to community service, a caring heart for people, and leadership roles at school and elsewhere are important to a prestigious college or university. High grades, high ACT/SAT scores (he might want to take a prep class or two), internships in particular fields of interest, and the ability to communicate easily both in person and on paper are also valuable.

If you and Luke have specific universities in mind already, check out the qualifications online together. If he sees them with his own eyes, and that university truly is his dream (not just yours), he'll be motivated to work even harder to get to where he wants to be.

All power to him!

Q: How are teachers certified, and what teaching credentials should they have?

A: Every state has different requirements for teacher education. They can also flex depending on how many years a teacher has invested in teaching and the locations where they have taught. If teachers are in specialty areas such as art, music, or faith classes, they don't have to be certified in some states. However, in general, most schools hire certified teachers—those with post–high school degrees (four years or more) in education.

The best way to check out the teachers is to read their bios, which most schools have posted on their website. The bios usually list whether the teachers have a BA, MA, or PhD; the institution the degree was received from; and how long they've been teaching.

Q: Anna's teacher has suggested that she repeat kindergarten. She says it's a readiness issue. But I don't understand. Anna's really bright and has always seemed ahead of others in her mental development. I'm not quite sure what to think, or whether to follow the teacher's recommendation. Your advice?

A: I understand how you feel. When my wife, Sande, came home from parent-teacher conferences and told me that our daughter Lauren's teacher had suggested she repeat kindergarten, my jaw dropped. "You're kidding," was all I said.

Lauren seemed bright from the very beginning. She was reading at a very young age. She could do mental gymnastics around any other child her age. But the teacher talked about her readiness being the big issue.

Having one of my kids repeat a grade was a hard pill for me to swallow. Maybe because I'd had so much experience with school failure myself as I was growing up.

Lauren's readiness had everything to do with her being the baby of our family but functionally an only child in the social aspect. She was born when Sande was turning 48 and I was turning 50. I was already going to be in my mid-60s when Lauren would be a senior in high school. Did we really want to make it one year more?

Sande and I looked at each other in shock. However, we loved Lauren's teacher and trusted her. She was a top-notch educator. So we followed her recommendation and held Lauren back a year.

Funny thing, Lauren ended up being at the top of her game throughout the rest of school. She thrived academically and vocationally and was a born leader. She won a writing contest in high school, started her own company, got scholarships in college and a top job with Disney Imagineering, and then nailed a coveted job at Hasbro.

Repeating kindergarten isn't a cardinal sin, though it might be a shock to you right now. Evaluate how ready you think your daughter is for kindergarten. Have another conference with your teacher and ask her for specifics.

Then do the wise thing. Give your kid the best start in life now by holding her back a year.

We never regretted it with Lauren. You won't either.

Individual Needs, Bents, and Talents

Q: My son's in a magnet school focusing on art, and I'm wondering whether to pull him out midsemester. He's always discouraged, saying he's not good enough, that everybody at school is better than he is. I tell him, "Honey, you're a great artist. You always have been," and remind him of things his grandparents have said about his artwork. But nothing I say seems to do any good. Would it be best to pull him out of that school?

A: Don't ever pull a kid out of a class or school midsemester, if you can help it. You're only teaching your child that when the going gets rough, he can quit and doesn't need to power through. That won't help him in challenges he faces in the future. If that art school was your son's idea and not yours, it's even more important that he stays. The rule should be, what a child chooses per semester (or per year in a schooling choice) needs to be what he sticks with. After the year is over, he can make a different choice. He needs to finish what he started.

Your son is in a slump because he's a perfectionist. Likely he's a firstborn or only child who thinks that if something doesn't turn out perfectly—the way he envisioned it to be— then it's a failure and he's a failure. True, he probably isn't the best artist. He's surrounded with talented kids at that school. A rule of life is, even if you're good at something, someone else is always better than you. At least that's the way it works in the real world, so why would it be any different in school? That's why he's not falling for your praise, because he knows it isn't true.

What he needs most right now is your encouragement. What's the difference?

Praise focuses on the child: "You're such a great artist." Encouragement focuses on the act: "Honey, it must feel really good to experiment with a new art genre. I know how much you've loved to paint since you were little. Tell me more about your painting."

An encourager doles out little bits and pieces of Vitamin E—Encouragement—just when the child needs it. You may not be sure what his painting represents, but you can honestly say, "I know you worked really hard on that today. I'd love to know where you got your ideas from."

Your son might not become Rembrandt reincarnated, but if he loves art and always has, this isn't the time he should change schools.

Q: My child has learning disabilities and physical disabilities. Besides the regular school factors, what should I consider?

A: Almost all schools have special education departments and staff who will set up an IEP (Individualized Education Plan) for your child. It will vary depending on your child's skill set. The most important criteria is, does the school welcome everyone coming through the door? Just because they have a program listed in their curriculum doesn't necessarily mean it's a focus for them or they are good at it.

Some schools are better at handling "differently abled" kids than others. This might be due to staffing or how much experience the school has in handling such programs. For example, has their program been in place 2 years or 12 years? Are their teachers certified in special ed? Do they have particular areas of specialty? One school might have a great program for visually impaired students. Another might be suited to handle physical impairments.

Look at the specific needs of your child and evaluate those needs through the grid of each of the schools you're considering.

Jonah, for example, was born with Down syndrome. Because the public school was close by and had a fabulous, long-lived program with compassionate teachers who specialized in handling such needs, his parents chose public school for morning classes. But because he showed interest in music and seemed to have an aptitude for it, he was a part of a community music program at a local college two afternoons a week and had a piano lesson with a special needs music instructor for one hour a week. On another afternoon he took PE at the same college with students who were training in physical therapy and offered a class for exceptional students.

Jonah's education is unusual but immensely creative and fits with his gifts. Kudos to his parents for pursuing the options and coming up with their own menu of educational success.

Parental Involvement

Q: My school has a PTO, but it seems like only the die-hard parents are involved. I'm not sure if I fit or can make the right kind of contribution. I want to be knowledgeable about what's going on in my kid's school and involved somehow. I really do care not only about my child but about the other kids in the school as well. Quality education is important to me, but so is making sure the environment is friendly and fun. Any tips?

A: You're already off on the right foot if quality education is important to you and you care about kids in general. You need to take a risk to get involved with the school because

232

the PTO needs people like you. If you don't try, how can you know if you can make a difference or not?

Many parents spend time complaining about the PTO or being scared of it instead of getting involved and working actively from within it. So why not be a contributor instead of sitting on the sidelines and wondering? Join the exchange of ideas, even if some of them are rather boring meetings. Be part of creating positive experiences at your school for the welfare of the kids, parents, faculty, and administration. The closer and healthier the partnership is between parents and the school, the better educational year your child will have.

Does that mean you have to quit your job to get involved? To volunteer to do things at school all the time?

No, but you should have an active interest in what the PTO is doing and contribute in ways that enrich the school. When you help set up art or science fairs or provide cookies for concerts, you're sharing your child's world and work and conveying that school is important to you too.

Q: I didn't do very well in school when I was growing up. It took years before I found my passion. How can I best help my son succeed where I failed? If I can spare him the pain of going through a bunch of years wondering, *Am I good at anything?* I want to do that.

A: You may feel like a failure, at least education-wise, but you're still the best teacher your child will ever have. You have something he doesn't—a healthy dose of experience. You know what didn't work in your schooling options. So let me ask you a question. In order for people to stay healthy, it's important for them to take vitamins, right? Well, in order for your child to live a healthy, well-balanced, successful life, what essential vitamins would you give him?

These are the ones I'd give him, for starters.

Vitamin A: Accountability. You always keep the tennis ball of life on the right side of the court. If it's his action, he's responsible and accountable for the consequences of it.

Vitamin B: Behavioral expectations. What you expect is what you get, so your expectations for honesty, trustworthiness, courtesy, respect, and hard work—as well as many other classic virtues—are always high.

Vitamin C: Cooperation. We truly are in life together, and we need each other. Sharing and getting along make the world go round.

Vitamin D: Discipline. Relational discipline is the name of the game—always loving and based on real-life consequences.

Vitamin E: Encouragement. Encouragement focuses on the act; praise focuses on the person. Encouragement reigns and lasts; praise is false and disappears like smoke in the wind.

Vitamin N: No. Are you always happy? Do you always get what you want? Then neither should he. Sometimes a little "No" is just what the doctor ordered.

Parents come in all shapes and sizes and backgrounds. Don't ever minimize your significance to your son. That "failure" was in the past. Now that you have long-term perspective, risk sharing some of the ups and downs of your own educational experiences. By doing so, you'll open your son's eyes to the importance of schooling and show him you have his best interests in mind. Best of all, you'll gain his heart.

School Environment

Q: Many schools I've checked out look good on the surface. But before I choose to get myself and my child involved with that school, how can I know if they're just putting a good face on their literature or they truly back what they say? Maybe I'm just suspicious by nature?

A: You're very wise to check out your options carefully before you leap. There's nothing like a personal visit to the school to help you make your decision. I believe it's very important to understand the heart of a school—especially since it's a place where your child will spend a lot of time—but that isn't something that easily translates on paper or the internet.

When you arrive at the school at the beginning of a school day, what do you see? Are teachers and administrators outside the classrooms, interacting warmly with students? Do they call them by their names and ask them questions that show they're aware of and engaged in the kids' lives? Or do the adults walk around as if they're all about the business, relating only to each other? In other words, does the school have heart and connection with the students, or is it heartless?

Do you see kids on the playground surrounding the principal and teachers?

When a magazine wanted to do a story on our school, their photographer asked me spontaneously, "Hey, I'd really like to get some kids pictured around you. Would that be possible?"

I smiled. "Watch this."

I beckoned him to walk with me toward the playground. Immediately, eight or nine kids ran toward me and surrounded me to give me hugs.

"Wow," the photographer said.

I grinned. "It's like that every day."

And it is. You know why? Because we care not only about education but about the whole person. We focus on core values of respect, concern for others, cooperation, honesty, dependability, and trustworthiness. The heart of our school is relationships. In fact, we even give out an encouragement award to the children who best model those core values.

As you observe adults and kids at the school and walk the hallways, ask yourself, *Is this a place where I'd like to spend eight hours every day? Where I could develop good relationships? Where people would care about me and I'd learn to care about others? Where I could get a quality education?*

If not, don't send your child there.

Q: I have four kids spaced several years apart, and I work part-time. My husband works full-time. We want our kids to get a good education, but we don't live relatively close to any schools we'd want to send them to. What should I consider in regard to the location of schools and transportation options?

A: I once thought about calling a book for moms *Help! I'm a Cabbie (and My SUV Isn't Even Yellow)*. If you feel like that in normal life with four kids, not even counting your part-time work and shuttling them back and forth to school, you've already got a lot going on. Especially since your kids span a wide age range. So here's some information to consider.

The public school that's maybe two miles down the road offers bus transportation to and from school. But in New

York, for example, your kid can go to a parochial school a mile from your home and also be picked up and dropped off by the public-school bus.

If your kids attend a private school of any kind, you're likely on your own for transportation. Either you drive your kid to school yourself or you ask about carpooling.

In general, it's best for parent and child if the school is relatively close to home. It's much easier for your child to make friends and have continuity with those friendships after school if you're not running all over town for playdates. So what do you do when you live on the northwest side of the city that's deteriorating, but you work in midtown?

Well, what schools do you drive by on the way to work that might be better for your child? Perhaps one of them has a great reputation and the qualities you're looking for. That choice seems to be a no-brainer. Yes, you'll have to drive to school every day and rearrange the beginning and end of your workday. But you drive right by the school, so there's no extra gas money spent or wear and tear on your already aging car.

With four kids, though, it can get tougher—especially if one of them has specific talents or special needs, which means other schooling options might be better. That's when the word *sacrifice* will take on all new meaning for you as a parent.

Yes, work is important, but your child's education, comfort level with the schooling option, and your relationship are the greater priority.

Work can be part of your life for a long time, even if it's at a different company, but you typically have your child with you for only 18 years. Why not make the best of those years and make sure your child has the right schooling match along the way?

Q: In the wake of all the school shootings, I'm worried about safety. Ever since a classmate brought a knife to school (even though it was a fake plastic knife for show-and-tell in first grade), I worry even more. The school has taken some precautions, but I wonder if it's enough. What can schools do, and what would you suggest?

A: Safety is a top priority at every school. Most schools have electronic barriers of some kind. Visitors have to enter the reception area first, then be buzzed in through electronic doors to get into the student area. Monitors patrol restrooms and hallways in shifts. Some schools have metal detectors that anyone entering the school has to walk through.

Schools also partner with local law enforcement and firefighters in surprise drills to test protocol and knowledge of their students, faculty, and staff.

At Leman Academy of Excellence, we do something else that's unique. We want to make sure we know everyone picking up and dropping off our younger children by name and face, so we meet our kids at the curb. Part of our safety protocol is that when cars pull up in the morning, a faculty or staff person takes the children by the hand and walks them into school. That way, if a car or individual shows up that isn't familiar to the faculty or staff, they're easy to spot. This is especially important today with single-parent or custody situations when children can become unwitting pawns in a power game between divorcing or ex-spouses.

Q: What's a good class size for the best learning potential? I don't want my child to get lost among a big number of students, but I don't want him to be only one of a few kids his age in a classroom either.

A: It depends on the school and the school's philosophy. Home schools can be very small, for example. There may be a limited number of kids the same age, if any. Public schools will have larger class sizes and a lot of peers. Private schools usually have minimum numbers for classes to stay afloat financially, and maximum numbers to keep parents happy.

But my personal view is that around 22 to 24 is a good class size for grades 1–12. For kindergarten, perhaps 20 max. Those class sizes allow the teacher to show attention to individual students.

However, along with the class size consideration is whether or not there are teacher's aides, and if so, how many. Having a teacher's aide in a classroom is really important, especially with kindergarteners and first graders. There is often a great difference in emotional and physical maturity and skill levels at those ages.

Another great idea that can allow for larger class sizes is having helpers—moms, dads, grandmas, grandpas, or other volunteer specialists—who come in as needed. Let's say a child needs extra help in reading. One of the helpers in the class volunteers to sit by that child and assist him with reading.

One private school I know of has a very special "Reluctant Reader" program for kindergarteners and first graders. Every Friday afternoon for an hour, a former teacher brings in her Saint Bernard, Luke, who used to be a water rescue dog with local firefighters. Five or six children who struggle with reading are chosen for a special time with Luke. The dog is gentle, loving, and perfectly happy to enjoy some strokes from the kids as they learn to read. When a child skips over a difficult word or doesn't form a word correctly, the teacher signals Luke to nudge the child so she looks back at the word and tries to say it again. It's a brilliant and creative plan that has now plunged five years' worth of reluctant readers at that school into the wonderful world of books.

Q: Homework makes our house a constant battlefield. Every night my 8-year-old gets frustrated with math. I try to help. She ends up crying and I get angry. I'm so sick of this drama. Help!

A: Ah, homework. There's little else that can turn a house into pure turmoil from 7:30 on. Even though your 8-year-old should be in bed by 9:00, she's still up by 11:00 and so overtired, it's no wonder she's having a meltdown. By that point, you aren't doing very well yourself and wish you were in front of the TV, watching *NCIS*.

Do yourself a favor. Stop helping . . . at least in that way. Save yourself a lot of grief and don't damage your relationship. Instead, find a high school kid who will come and do one hour of tutoring after school Monday through Thursday. It could be someone you know from the neighborhood. Because it's just an hour, it won't cost you a lot of money, but it's consistent. Subjects like math need that kind of consistency, not just once a week. What gets learned on Monday needs to get re-formed on Tuesday, solidified on Wednesday, and finalized on Thursday.

If you don't do something different, nothing will change. The wail of "It's too hard!" will be cemented in your ears. Your child is past the point where she wants to listen to you. Plus your pattern is set. When you get frustrated enough, you end up doing her homework for her.

So, my question is, who is the organ grinder and who is the monkey?

Your daughter may be frustrated with math, but she's getting you to do the work for her. She won't learn that way. You both need to break the pattern. Introducing someone else who is good at math (and with whom she won't melt down) is a great idea. So is having her tutoring time when she's fresh, and it's not past her usual bedtime.

Your role? To stay out of the kitchen, where the tutoring is taking place. When the work is done, the tutor has gone, and your child is smiling, you say, "Wow, that must feel great to get your work done so fast. Now look at all the free time you have."

You can smile too. Your daughter has learned to finish what she starts and to do her own work. You've regained your sanity for just a few shekels a week.

Not a bad deal.

Q: My son, Sean, had a terrible last year. He was ill with pneumonia and missed over five weeks of school. His best friend moved away between semesters. Sean was born in September, so he's one of the younger kids in his sixth-grade class. I'm wondering what your thoughts would be about moving him to another school to give him a fresh start, and also keeping him in the sixth grade.

A: You ought to hang up your shingle as a psychologist, because you already have a pretty good sense of what should happen. Your son's had a rough year physically and emotionally. He was sick and gone from class, then lost his BFF. That's a lot for anybody to manage within nine months—no matter whether they are 11 or 35.

I agree with you. You ought to give him a fresh start— both at school and by having a do-over on sixth grade. He probably feels behind anyway, and since he's young, no one at his new school would have a clue he's repeating a grade unless he tells them. Attending a different school also gives him the opportunity to be on an even playing field to gain new friends.

There are all kinds of schooling options today, so he might even want to attend a completely different type of school. The fresh start in itself should be an encouragement to him, if you present the message positively. "Sean, you've had quite a year, huh? You're a good student, but you missed so much after your bout with pneumonia. I know you feel like you've really fallen behind, and you're discouraged. Well, I have a suggestion. Since Matt moved and got a new start, let's give you one too.

"You know about the academy down the road, right? I've done some checking, and it might be a perfect schooling option for you. I'm willing to drive you the three miles every day so you can have a fresh start. I want you to have an awesome next year in school. That's why I think it would be smart for you to be in sixth grade again. You'll have a jump start on learning the subjects, and this time you'll be one of the oldest kids in the class instead of the youngest."

I know being one of the oldest kids sounds like a little thing, but it's really a big one, especially for boys. If he's athletic, that's another plus. In sixth grade, even a few months in age between boys can make a huge difference in physical development. If your son is older and more mature, he has a competitive edge that will boost his confidence and his leadership skills.

Now that's a win-win combination.

Q: I'm debating whether to put my child in half-day or full-day kindergarten. Many of my friends say all day is the best option after preschool—to introduce kids to the length of a "regular school" before they head into academic pressure in first grade. But I'm not sure all day is the right option for my son, who just turned 5 in October. Your thoughts?

A: I'll start my answer with a question to you. What kind of impact do you want to have on your son's life?

When children are young, time spent with you, especially unpressured time, is critically important. There will be lots of years where others will influence his life—including multiple teachers and coaches in his academic career—but the type of relationship you two establish in the early years influences greatly who your child becomes and how you will relate to each other even as adults.

If you are vacillating between the two options, it's always better to go with the one that represents less time away from you.

Then again, many parents work outside the home today. They have to go out the door early and don't arrive home until late, especially if they commute longer distances to work. Many kindergarteners are dropped off at 6:30 a.m., even if kindergarten doesn't start until 9:00 and is over at noon. The kids eat the sack lunch prepared by their parent, then go to aftercare for the afternoon, and Mom or Dad picks them up around 6:00 or 7:00 p.m.

That's an awfully long day for a young kid. For such kids, it's no surprise that school isn't a fun place to be. Mom isn't there, Dad isn't there, and it's not home.

To accommodate working parents, Leman Academy of Excellence has both half-day and full-day kindergarten options, but I have a strong bias for half-day kindergarten. Young kids have pretty short attention spans. They need time both to interact socially and to play quietly by themselves. They need to develop perspectives on others (giving, sharing, connecting), but they also need one-on-one time with Mom and Dad to develop self-worth and confidence.

If you're a working-outside-the-home parent, anything you can do to go for a half-day option is best. Call in the grandparents or your sister to help. Rearrange your work schedule or shorten your hours. Take another mom's kid under your wing for three hours every Friday afternoon, and let her do the same for you every Thursday afternoon.

Choosing the right schooling options at the right time, based on the maturity level and needs of your child, is a balancing act.

Then again, so is everything about parenting.

Q: Chelsea, my daughter, used to have a BFF at middle school. Now she says, "I hate her." I have no idea what happened, but they don't hang out anymore. Now Chelsea doesn't seem to have any friends. Should I try a different school? Or just wait it out?

A: Welcome to the land of emotions. As my wife says, "An 11-year-old girl is the worst creature on the planet." In these tumultuous years, phrases like "I hate you" are flung with volume and regularity.

The overreacting mom will say, "Oh, honey, you don't mean that. Why would you say something like that? We don't talk like that in our family."

But what have you just done? Sat over her in judgment like King Solomon. Is that really what you want to do?

One of the best things you can do is just listen when she's ready to talk. Memorize the words "Tell me more about that." Even though the phrase is a command in the English language, it doesn't raise your child's defenses like asking her questions does. It communicates that you're interested.

Kids this age will have a BFF one minute and an enemy the next. The winds of change are always in tornado mode, so nothing lasts for long. There is little loyalty in the peer group. Sometimes all it takes for a friendship to end is one girl telling another, "You have an ugly nose." Worse, she likes the same boy her friend does. Kids are so insecure in middle school that one of the ways they make themselves feel better is by putting other people down.

There's also an old mantra that's applicable here: "Same person, same setting, same outcome. Same person, different setting, same outcome." It usually takes two to tango, so it's highly probable that Chelsea contributed to the friend breakup. Even if she gains a new friend, if she says or does the same thing she did before, she might lose this one.

The wise mom might turn this event into a teachable lesson by gently prompting her daughter. "You seem sad and angry to have lost Shelli as a friend. I don't know what happened between you two, but I know you'll figure it out. Sometimes we say things we don't mean, and they can really hurt other people."

Note that you didn't ask Chelsea what, if anything, she did. You just dropped the seed of an idea into her mind that she can choose to pursue. Whether she does or not will tell you a lot about her maturity level in navigating relationships.

What can you do in the midst of these winds of change?

Years ago, when people flew on certain airplanes, there would be a pilot, a copilot, and a navigator on board, whose job was to make sure the plane was navigating the skies in the right way. You are the navigator for the airplane that bears your daughter's name.

So stay calm and navigate on.

Q: Some schools require uniforms. Others don't. What's your view, and why?

A: I like uniforms because they put every scholar on the same footing. Whether you're wealthy or dirt poor, whether your parents are professionals who work in fancy offices downtown or recent immigrants from Peru, whether you live with your stepparents in a five-bedroom home with the latest amenities or your 1,000-square-foot house that always smells a little like wet dog fur because your mom is a veterinarian . . . put on a uniform and everybody who walks through the doors of the school looks the same to everybody else. All then have equal opportunities at school. Clothes can't make the difference in someone's perception of you.

That's why Leman Academy of Excellence has a uniform. It's not one of the fancy ones you would have at a parochial school. We just specify a couple of colors for shirts—say, plain polos with no writing (the inexpensive Old Navy/Kohl's variety)—and khaki pants. We have dress-down Fridays so kids can wear whatever they want, except anything with wording. We also have fun with the dress code, loosening it up through special fun days such as "Dress Up Like Your Favorite Cartoon Character" or "Dress Up Like the Vocation You Want to Be Someday."

The point is, many schools have students on extreme ends of the financial spectrum and lots of students in the middle. I believe it's important for scholars to learn how to interact with the diverse world we live in—and that includes all kinds of people. When those with more wealth meet those with less, they become more aware of what they have, consider the opportunity to choose how to spend it, and can become givers rather than takers. When those with less wealth meet those with more, they have the opportunity to break stereotypes that may exist, such as "All rich kids are snotty."

Uniforms go a long way toward leveling the playing field so that everybody can form a team to play the same game.

Social Interaction and Peers

Q: My daughter just entered middle school, and all of a sudden she has not only a different circle of friends but completely different types of friends—the kind of people she wouldn't necessarily have hung out with before. I'm a little worried. Should I be?

A: First of all, when children change schools, their friends will change. If she went to the same elementary school all her childhood, changing schools may be a first experience for both of you. Middle schools draw from different areas of town. All of a sudden a new and exciting mix of kids is in your daughter's life. They're not the same kids she grew up with and who all had braces together, whose parents you knew a lot about because you saw them on the playground and at school events for years.

Now you're listening to your daughter talk about new kids—you've never heard their names before and know nothing about their parents or home life. Understandably, you're a little concerned, because these new people are potential influencers in your kid's life—especially at a time where she's beginning to discover who she is and what her talents are apart from you as a parent.

There's an easy solution. You can play it smart. Say to your daughter, "Wow, that's great you're making new friends. They're welcome here anytime. In fact, I'm going to make cookies for us tomorrow. If your friends are around, I'll make an extra big batch. Or you guys could just eat cookie dough while I'm baking."

Your daughter perks up. After all, there's no better draw for hungry adolescents than food, nor does a place feel more like home than if it has heavenly aromas.

"I've got a great idea," she says with enthusiasm. "Would it be okay with you if a couple of them come home with me tomorrow? Could you run them home if we hang out here for a few hours?"

You smile broadly. Mission accomplished. "Sure. No problem."

248

Note that you didn't tell your daughter, "Hey, I'd love to meet your friends. Why don't you have them over sometime?" That might have been a tip-off to your daughter that you'll be checking them out.

When those kids show up, spend a little time in the kitchen with them. You can bake cookies and clean up *slowly*, you know. After a little time overhearing their natural conversation, you'll have a good feel for these new friends—how they treat each other, what they talk about, etc.

Q: My daughter does well in school—she's a B student—but not as good as I think she can do. Even she admits she doesn't study very much. She'd rather do things with friends or surf the latest music releases on the web. Knowing what I do about how college can influence your life positively, how can I motivate her to care more about her grades?

A: There's double good news for you. First, your daughter is pulling decent grades, not bad ones. Lots of parents would be jumping up and down in a delirium of joy if their child came home with all Bs on their report card. Second, your daughter has already admitted herself that she doesn't study much, so she's tuned in to her own study habits.

There are many parents like you who have bright kids who bring home Bs but could easily get As. They're smart and articulate, and they do well in life in general. But often they'd rather major in people and a social life and minor in subjects like calculus and biology. So they do enough to get by.

Let's be honest. You can't *make* your kid do anything. But you can also set up situations where your daughter figures out, "Hey, if I get better grades, it might affect my future."

Maybe it's time for an honest and upbeat talk with your winsome daughter that will give her a little taste of reality.

"Honey, there's a lot going on this time of year, and I know you're really busy. I realize your biology teacher is boring and hard to listen to. I admit I nearly fell asleep at parent-teacher conferences. But I wanted to share with you something he told me—that you're very good at grasping the intricacies of biology.

"I know you're interested in pursuing genetics potentially as a career. Biology's an important part of that. Someday people will decide whether or not to admit you into a genetics program in college based on your grades. I'm just wondering if you think the B they'll see in biology presents a true picture of who you really are and what you can do in that field."

Sharing such thoughts might introduce a needed perspective to your daughter. Sometimes children are more motivated if they see that they might get something in return.

But you, parent, also need to keep something in mind. Right now you're talking to a kid, not the provost of a university. She can't fully grasp what you already know and have been through. So before you push your child too hard, remember how you were at that age. Listing the top 10 songs on the Top 40 list in order was probably a lot more fun than reading about the Magna Carta, wasn't it?

Your push to give your child a better life is a good thing, as long as you don't push too hard. Your daughter still needs time to be what she is—a teenager.

Q: I got a call yesterday from my son's teacher, who informed me that Brandon has been bullying other kids. I had to pick him up from the principal's office. Evidently the playground monitor had been watching him, and this time he'd pushed another boy off the swing.

I couldn't believe it. At first I thought, *No way can this be my son. Brandon's always been a good kid. Sure, he gets angry every once in a while, but he's never been mean to others.* But when I got to the principal's office, I found out the truth. It was written all over Brandon's face.

Recently I got divorced. My son and I moved into an apartment, and he had to switch schools. Maybe all the changes and stress have been too much for him? Should I keep him at home? Find a different school? I'm shocked and embarrassed.

A: Any parent who gets a call like that from a teacher needs to take it seriously and adopt the stance that the teacher is right. Most schools have step-by-step procedures they have to follow with such happenings.

No, that action might not resemble anything close to what your child has done in the past. It's not a natural thing for any parent to admit, "Yeah, my child did that." But in this kind of situation, you have to shut your mouth and listen to what the teacher and principal have to say—even with details you really don't want to hear and that might shock you to the core. You don't make excuses, such as, "Well, I just went through a divorce."

Yes, it might be stressful at home right now, but your child chose to act inappropriately. He needs to experience some reality discipline—being confronted with the full truth of what he did. You, the protector of your child, need to allow him to face the proverbial music. You can't rescue him from the consequences.

If the principal hasn't arranged for it already, suggest a meeting with all parties involved—the other child and his or her parents, you and your child, the principal, and the teacher. If all parties are in the room at the same time, the playing ground is level and there's no "he said, she said" to cause later misunderstandings.

If children are young, a simple "let's shake hands and be friends" will often work to resolve the matter. But if there are any physical issues that result—for example, the other boy got hurt falling off the swing—this is a more serious matter, especially if the other parents are sue-happy. That, parent, isn't a place you want to be. So you need to nip this behavior in the bud right now, before it has the opportunity to progress.

In the upcoming meeting, at the very least, both sides deserve to hear all the details of what happened. Was anything said prior to the swing incident that sparked your son's behavior? When kids get into trouble, the other side usually isn't completely innocent.

What does Brandon need from you right now? Some loving direct talk.

"You know I love you, right?" you ask.

He nods sheepishly.

"But you also know that what you did was inappropriate, right?" you continue.

He nods again.

"Can you think of other things you could have said or done that would have been a lot better than what you did?"

"Yes," he says meekly.

"Like what?" you ask, then hear his brainstorms and say, "Yes, those would be better ideas."

Will something like this happen again? Possibly. Kids are kids. But they need to adhere not only to the conduct rules of the school but to what is kind, moral, and right. You never hit others or push them around.

Because of all the changes Brandon has been through recently, he might benefit from talking to a trusted adult who understands children of divorce. His lashing out at the other child might very well be his way of trying to control something about his life. He may feel guilt for his mom and dad's marriage falling apart and wonder if it's his fault.

Yes, this situation is shocking and embarrassing. But it's also a wake-up call for you, because it's your son's cry for help. You need to pay attention and get him that help sooner rather than later.

Q: I grew up in a public school. I still live in the same neighborhood, but the area has changed a lot since I was young. Part of me would like my kids to go to the same school I did, but I'm not sure it's the right thing. Everybody keeps telling me I should be concerned about keeping my child away from the "bad public school kids." Some of my friends are sending their kids to private schools, but we don't have the money for that. Should I consider homeschooling?

A: Keeping your kids away from the "bad public school kids" is absolutely the worst reason to choose to homeschool. Yet I hear it from parents all the time. Interestingly, many parents who have been passionate about homeschooling and carried that responsibility for years now have children who attend Leman Academy. You see, homeschoolers

253

- love having input in their child's education, and I'm all about encouraging parents to partner in that with teachers and administration
- like the idea that children are not the center of the universe but are a part of a universe—the way a family is set up
- want to rear respectful, kind, well-behaved children who can stand firm on their morals and values

When those longtime homeschooling parents walked into a second-grade class at Leman Academy, the teacher asked the class, "What kind of class are you?"

The chorus of answers was simultaneous: "A respectful class!"

Other classes might tell you, "A kind class!"

The homeschooling parents were shocked. Why? Because Leman Academy is a charter school—a *public* school—with a very diverse makeup of students. Yet we emphasize the same virtues that are important to homeschooling parents.

Maybe public school kids aren't always "bad kids" after all.

Your kids will meet all kinds of people in life. They'll come in different shapes, sizes, faiths, ethnicities, and nationalities. And you know what's interesting and wonderful? Every single person has been created by God Almighty. That means all people are deserving of love, respect, belonging, and acceptance.

Now, do we like everything about those people? No.

Their sometimes crass language and obnoxious behavior? No.

Their lifestyle that's a far cry from ours? No.

But we still have to respect them, which means never being in a position where you talk down to anyone. Boys and girls, men and women, rich and poor, and everyone in between—all are of equal value.

So if a classmate flings verbal insults, you teach your child that she should respond in kindness and with self-control, then walk away with head held high. Not because the other person deserves that kindness and even tone, but because it's a reflection of who your child is and who you've reared her to be in your family. The more practice your child has in relating with others in such a way, the stronger her ability will be to stand against any of life's pressures.

How you respond to people who are different from you—and might be as annoying as all heck—determines the kind of impact you will have not only on that person as an individual but on the world in general. People who are respectful, kind, honest, and hardworking are rare in today's world and therefore make a very powerful statement to those around them just by being who they are.

Now, if you can just translate what your child is learning about kindness to that driver next to you on the expressway . . . before you lay on the horn.

Q: Nikki, my second-grade daughter, came home crying because another girl in the class told her she was fat. That made me really angry. Yes, my daughter is a little on the chunky side—I also was growing up—but that doesn't mean someone has the right to bully her. Nikki shouldn't have to put up with that at school. How should I handle it? Get the teacher involved? Call the other parent?

A: Hold it right there before you switch to an even higher gear. No one likes to be called fat, whether they have a little extra around the middle, like me, or not. Parents especially don't like anyone (other than themselves) picking on their little angel.

However, just because the other girl said something negative to Nikki doesn't mean the other girl is a bully. I hate to be the bearer of bad news, but kids have historically been unkind to each other. It's a fact. Kids say blunt things. They don't sugarcoat anything; they call a spade a spade. They also do colossally stupid things, like sticking their tongue on a frozen pipe (been there, done that). It's all a part of growing up.

Another part of growing up is what I call "developing psychological muscles" to deal with the cheap shots of life you get from your peer group.

A single incident isn't necessarily bullying. The definition of bullying is

- repeated and excessive badgering of a child (not a one-time offense)
- an uneven "me against you" (a much larger or older child picking on a smaller or younger child)
- a group against an individual

Behavior that meets those stipulations should never be tolerated in school—ever. But not every negative incident is bullying.

Most often, kids put others down to feel better about themselves. They say vicious things about classmates out of jealousy, anger, or boredom.

If the other girl has repeatedly behaved like this, yes, she is a bully and should be dealt with appropriately through the rules of school conduct. Or she may have simply, in kid fashion, called a spade a spade. Perhaps your daughter does weigh more than others in the class. Since you grew up with weight being a hot button, it's no wonder someone saying it to your daughter makes you angry, and you're in mama bear protective mode.

However, if you really want your daughter to excel socially and also grow her psychological muscles, you'll realize other things may be going on.

Children love to overexaggerate events, especially if they know they can raise a ruckus with you. If this is a onetime event, do you really want to raise the roof by contacting the teacher, the principal, and the other parent? Or can you use this as a life lesson to your daughter on how to respond better emotionally when someone lobs a negative shot her way?

Children also love to tell only one side of the story. If you got both children in a room and put them under a heat lamp with their teacher, would Nikki admit to saying something unkind too? A word or two that might even have prompted the "you're fat" comment? Be aware that what you hear isn't always the whole story.

Q: I grew up in a small town. I didn't have to worry much about peer pressure, since everybody in town knew what you were doing. If you did something your mom shouldn't know about, someone told her anyway, and you never did it again.

I married later in life and gained two stepdaughters I love deeply. The world they're growing up in (we all live in a city now) is completely different. When I see all the pressures they face, I worry. I don't want my girls to grow up as fast as they seem to be. Maybe it's just the protective dad in me, but I worry that they'll be exposed to too much too early. Now that they're teenagers and more out on their own, what's the best way to keep them safe at school and their extracurricular activities?

A: Unless you are God Almighty, you can't keep your girls completely safe. They have to live in the real world, not in a bubble that you construct for them. They will hear language that isn't good, watch things that make them uncomfortable, and even find themselves in potentially dangerous situations.

But here's the upside to that truth. You, Dad, are the best antidote to anything negative that might happen. Here's why. If you have the kind of close relationship with your daughters that it seems you do, then start a little conversation with them.

"You know how much I love you two, right?" you say.

They nod.

"Well, sometimes you'll be in situations where things will turn a little scary. You'll get an inner nudge of, *Uh-oh, something is going down here, and I don't like the direction it's headed.* When that happens, get out of there as fast as you can. Call me immediately, tell me where you are, and I'll come get you. No questions asked."

Your girls are at an age where, when things go south, they go south in a hurry. If your daughters worry about where they are or what you might think, they may stay longer in that situation than they should and incur additional risk.

How do I know that conversation works to protect your kids? Because I had the same one with each of my five kids.

Sometimes I did get calls, and I went and picked up my kids, no questions asked. I didn't pressure them later either. At times they gave me the skinny on what happened. Many times I didn't know until years later, when the truth came out around the Thanksgiving dinner table. For some of the events, I still don't know what happened.

As my kids say, "Dad, there are some things you should never know."

I heartily agree. I can sleep better not knowing. To this day, I still haven't asked why they were where they were on those occasions. What matters most is that my kids trusted me and called when they needed me.

You see, it's all about the relationship.

If your girls trust you, they'll call you . . . especially if you don't ask questions.

AN ENCOURAGING WORD

There's an old tune I love called "She Believes in Me," sung by Kenny Rogers. Though the lyrics talk about the faithful support of a spouse, I think of my mother every time I hear those words.

It's always been amazing to me how deep a mother's love can be—even when, quite frankly, I didn't give my mother an awful lot of reason or empirical evidence to believe in me as I was growing up. Yet she did anyway. She had my back, even when, for years, traditional teachers incessantly drummed into her head this mantra: "If Kevin would only apply himself, he could succeed."

Well, I did succeed—just not in the way anyone at my old schools would have expected, and I had a slow start. In fact, it's funny. As you move closer to death, people in institutions offer you things like honorary doctorate degrees and achievement awards. You receive accolades from students you've taught and other people whose lives have touched yours in one way or another.

One of the ceremonial events I couldn't turn down was returning to my old high school. I had the tremendous privilege of taking my 90-year-old mother with me to sit by my side. As we sat together, we reminisced. I reminded her of all the mischief I had gotten into as a kid.

Like the time I was 3 years old and got away from her in church. When she lost her grip on me, I became like a mole on the floor. In those days, women would take their shoes off when they were sitting in the pews. I thought it was rather amusing to take Mrs. Anderson's pair and switch it with someone else's. One of the pairs was in row five and the other in row three. Just imagine these women, at the last hymn of the service, getting up and trying to put their shoes on. My mother was so embarrassed. Little Cubby Leman was up to mischief again.

Or the time I was so bored at school that I decided to create a little excitement. I started a fire in the teacher's garbage can. It was only one of my many antics.

I think my mother was in the principal's office more than I was because I skipped school so much.

No matter what I came up with, Mom nodded and said, "Oh, I do remember that. You scalawag, you. But you were such a good boy."

You were such a good boy. To this day, those words so often spoken by my mother still ring in my ears. Now, that's a mother's love for her kids. Love can sure be blind, can't it?

My saintly mother did admit that when I was about 3 years old, she once put me in a harness attached to a steel line that stretched between a maple and an elm tree in our yard. I was like a dog on a run.

Later in life, I had fun telling my mother's friends that she'd tied me to a dog run. Out of the blue I'd say, "What did she think I was—part Weimaraner?"

Mom would laugh like crazy. "If I didn't," she'd say, "you'd run away. I never knew where you were."

I was always on the go. My mom had good reason to worry about my safety.

Yes, Kevin Leman was mischievous and a "scalawag," to quote Mom. I still am to this day. In fact, when my buddy Moonhead and I are together, my wife often tells us to act our age.

When I was a kid, I didn't care a whit about education. I saw no place for it in my life. My fishing pole held much more intrigue and higher acclaim than my seat in the classroom.

> My saintly mother did admit that when I was about 3 years old, she once put me in a harness attached to a steel line that stretched between a maple and an elm tree in our yard. I was like a dog on a run.

My parents faced numerous challenges in my growing-up years and early twenties in regard to my cavalier attitude about education. Yet here I am years later, a champion of education with multiple degrees and the founder of a school with my name on it.

You too will face challenges along the way in your child's education. Things won't always go as you planned. Your child will fail in small and large ways. But your belief in her—yes, even if all evidence is to the contrary—will make all the difference in her eventual life success.

I'll say it again. On the menu of education, you, parent, are the main dish. All other options are a la carte choices that you can mix and match for your particular child. But no one else can replace that main dish in their lives.

The best education of all comes from you. Yes, it's a lot of hard work and responsibility. But it has lifetime benefits for both of you—the most rewarding one, your relationship.

TOP 10 LIST

What to Look For in a Quality Education

1. It has a warm, safe setting with faculty and staff who care individually about student welfare.

2. It has challenging academics with real-life application.

3. It covers well the four basics (math, science, history, English) but allows for exploration of talents.

4. It provides a healthy balance of respect, responsibility, accountability, and discipline.

5. It allows for differences in learning styles, personalities, and gifts.

6. It employs teachers who are qualified, certified, and cutting-edge in their field.

7. It's a place where a love for learning is obvious and encouragement reigns.

8. It's a classroom where uniqueness and diversity are encouraged and applauded.

9. It's a school where parental participation and partnership are welcomed.

10. It's a fun, interactive environment so the child loves being there!

NOTES

Introduction

1. Kate Zernike, "Test Scores Show a Decline in Math among High School Seniors," *New York Times*, April 27, 2016, http://www.nytimes.com/2016/04/27/us/math-test-scores-decline-high-school-seniors.html?_r=0.

2. Marten Roorda, quoted in "ACT Scores Down for 2016 U.S. Grad Class Due to Increased Percentage of Students Tested," ACT, August 24, 2016, http://www.act.org/content/act/en/newsroom/act-scores-down-for-2016-us-grad-class-due-to-increased-percentage-of-students-tested.html.

3. William J. Bennett, quoted in Intercollegiate Studies Institute, *Choosing the Right College: The Whole Truth about America's Top Schools*, rev. and exp. ed. (Grand Rapids: Eerdmans, 2001), xiii.

Chapter 1 The Top Concerns of Parents

1. Sherry Towers, Andres Gomez-Lievano, Maryam Khan, Anuj Mubayi, and Carlos Castillo-Chavez, "Contagion in Mass Killings and School Shootings," PLOS ONE, July 2, 2015, http://journals.plos.org/plosone/article?id=10.1371/journal.pone.0117259.

2. "Hard Lessons in School Safety," Security Today, October 27, 2015, https://securitytoday.com/blogs/reaction/2015/10/Hard-Lessons-in-School-Safety.aspx.

3. Ibid.

4. William J. Bennett, quoted in "Demand for Excellence," *New York Times*, September 3, 1986, http://www.nytimes.com/1986/09/03/us /demand-for-excellence.html.

Chapter 2 Factoring In Your Child's Uniqueness

1. Overview of Learning Styles, Learning-Styles-Online.com, accessed October 1, 2016, http://www.learning-styles-online.com/overview.

Chapter 3 Schooling a la Carte

1. A Beka Academy, http://www.abekaacademy.org.

ABOUT DR. KEVIN LEMAN

An internationally known psychologist, radio and television personality, speaker, educator, and humorist, **Dr. Kevin Leman** has taught and entertained audiences worldwide with his wit and commonsense psychology.

The *New York Times* bestselling and award-winning author of over 50 titles, including *The Birth Order Book, Have a New Kid by Friday*, and *Sheet Music*, has made thousands of house calls through radio and television programs, including *FOX & Friends, The Real Story, The View*, FOX's *The Morning Show, Today, Morning in America, The 700 Club*, CBS's *The Early Show, Janet Parshall*, CNN, and *Focus on the Family*. Dr. Leman has served as a contributing family psychologist to *Good Morning America* and frequently speaks to schools, CEO groups, and businesses, including Fortune 500 companies and others such as YPO, Million Dollar Round Table, and Top of the Table.

Dr. Leman's professional affiliations include the American Psychological Association, SAG-AFTRA, and the North American Society of Adlerian Psychology. He received the

Distinguished Alumnus Award (1993) and an honorary Doctor of Humane Letters degree (2010) from North Park University; and a bachelor's degree in psychology, and later his master's and doctorate degrees, as well as the Alumni Achievement Award (2003), from the University of Arizona.

For 10 years he taught graduate courses in education and applied psychology at the University of Arizona and was the assistant dean of students. He also worked for a year there as the assistant director of high school relations, helping students in their life mapping—identifying strengths and weaknesses and fine-tuning career directions. For years, he has spoken frequently nationwide at schools and conferences about his own experiences in education, why a good education is critical to life success, and how to build healthy dynamics between parent and child as they seek long-term goals together.

Dr. Leman is the founder and chairman of the board of Leman Academy of Excellence (www.lemanacademy .com), which is based on his time-tested principles of family, birth order, respect, and accountability. In its first year of operation, Leman Academy of Excellence was voted the top charter school in Tucson, Arizona, through the Readers' Choice Awards (*Arizona Daily Star*). Leman Academy willingly engages and embraces parents in the educational process and is founded on the key principle that parental involvement is essential in maximizing the student's educational experience. Dr. Leman's passion to provide a different type of education—pursuing excellence as an ultimate goal for a lifetime while preparing for real-life skills—is based on his own story of struggling through school until he found his unique niche.

Dr. Leman's passion is to change the conversation that happens every day across America, between parents and children, about what they learned in school.

Originally from Williamsville, New York, Dr. Leman and his wife, Sande, live in Tucson, Arizona, and have five children and four grandchildren.

If you're looking for an entertaining speaker for your event or fund-raiser, or for information regarding business consultations, webinars, or the annual "Wit and Wisdom" cruise, please contact:

Dr. Kevin Leman
P.O. Box 35370
Tucson, Arizona 85740
Phone: (520) 797-3830
Fax: (520) 797-3809
www.birthorderguy.com
www.drleman.com

Follow Dr. Kevin Leman on Facebook (facebook.com /DrKevinLeman) and on Twitter (@DrKevinLeman). Check out the free podcasts at birthorderguy.com/podcast.

RESOURCES BY DR. KEVIN LEMAN

Nonfiction Books for Adults

The Birth Order Book
Have a New Kid by Friday
Have a New Husband by Friday
Have a New Teenager by Friday
The Way of the Shepherd (written with William Pentak)
Have a New You by Friday
Have a New Sex Life by Friday
Have a Happy Family by Friday
Planet Middle School
The Way of the Wise
Be the Dad She Needs You to Be
What a Difference a Mom Makes
Parenting the Powerful Child
Under the Sheets
Sheet Music
Making Children Mind without Losing Yours
It's Your Kid, Not a Gerbil!

Born to Win

Sex Begins in the Kitchen

7 Things He'll Never Tell You . . . But You Need to Know

What Your Childhood Memories Say about You

Running the Rapids

Becoming the Parent God Wants You to Be

Becoming a Couple of Promise

A Chicken's Guide to Talking Turkey with Your Kids about Sex (written with Kathy Flores Bell)

First-Time Mom

Step-parenting 101

Living in a Stepfamily without Getting Stepped On

The Perfect Match

Be Your Own Shrink

Stopping Stress before It Stops You

Single Parenting That Works

Why Your Best Is Good Enough

Smart Women Know When to Say No

Fiction: The Worthington Destiny Series, with Jeff Nesbit

A Perfect Ambition

A Powerful Secret

A Primary Decision

Books for Children, with Kevin Leman II

My Firstborn, There's No One Like You

My Middle Child, There's No One Like You

My Youngest, There's No One Like You
My Only Child, There's No One Like You
My Adopted Child, There's No One Like You
My Grandchild, There's No One Like You

DVD/Video Series for Group Use

Have a New Kid by Friday
Making Children Mind without Losing Yours (parenting edition)
Making Children Mind without Losing Yours (public school teacher edition)
Value-Packed Parenting
Making the Most of Marriage
Running the Rapids
Single Parenting That Works
Bringing Peace and Harmony to the Blended Family

DVDs for Home Use

Straight Talk on Parenting
Why You Are the Way You Are
Have a New Husband by Friday
Have a New You by Friday
Have a New Kid by Friday

Available at 1-800-770-3830 • www.birthorderguy.com • www.drleman.com

Kid-tested,
parent-approved

If anyone understands why children behave the way they do, it's Dr. Kevin Leman. In this bestseller he equips parents with seven principles of reality discipline—a loving, no-nonsense parenting approach that really works.

Revell
a division of Baker Publishing Group
www.RevellBooks.com

Available wherever books and ebooks are sold.

You are about to embark on a fantastic journey.

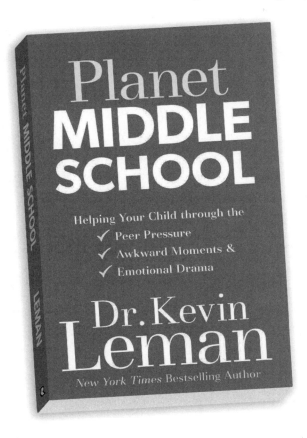

Middle schoolers can be a strange, unpredictable species. But with a little help from Dr. Kevin Leman, you can ride out the interstellar storm with humor and confidence. He will show you how you can help your child not only survive but thrive during these turbulent years.

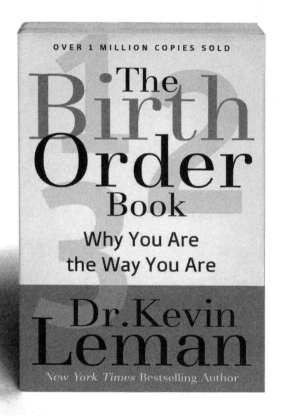

Powerful kids don't just happen…
THEY'RE CREATED.

Whether loud and temperamental, quiet and sensitive, or stubborn and manipulative, powerful children can make living with them a challenge. But it doesn't have to be that way.